A Funny Thing Happened on My Way to Freedom

Desi Sanchez

iUniverse, Inc.
Bloomington

A FUNNY THING HAPPENED ON MY WAY TO FREEDOM

iUniverse books may be ordered through booksellers or by contacting:

iUniverse
1663 Liberty Drive
Bloomington, IN 47403
www.iuniverse.com
1-800-Authors (1-800-288-4677)

Because of the dynamic nature of the Internet, any web addresses or links contained in this book may have changed since publication and may no longer be valid. The views expressed in this work are solely those of the author and do not necessarily reflect the views of the publisher, and the publisher hereby disclaims any responsibility for them.

Any people depicted in stock imagery provided by Thinkstock are models, and such images are being used for illustrative purposes only.

Certain stock imagery © Thinkstock.

ISBN: 978-1-4759-5520-0 (sc)
ISBN: 978-1-4759-5522-4 (hc)
ISBN: 978-1-4759-5521-7 (e)

Library of Congress Control Number: 2012921075

Printed in the United States of America

iUniverse rev. date: 11/8/2012

To my family, friends, and schoolmates; my crewmates on the SS *Houston*; the 2506 Brigade; and the crew members of the DDE-510 USS *Eaton*.

Table of Contents

Acknowledgments

I give my sincere thanks to all my family members and friends for their encouragement in the writing of this true story.

Prologue

I wrote, back in 1964, a quick account of my life in Havana, as well my experiences in the Bay of Pigs Invasion of April 17, 1961. At the time of this writing, I had never given a thought to the notion that the Bay of Pigs would become a subject taught at the high school level—a part of American history, as well as Cuban history.

My original notes were specifically about the invasion, but if my book was going to be an account of my life, then how I got to that point must also be told. I started my story at age twelve, with a Mother's Day celebration; coincidentally it was May 12, 1951. That day, I was with my father, and a few minutes later, we had a car accident that left my face scarred.

Then I told of my first love, with a very unattainable dream girl; I assure you that was not my first rejection. I spent my college years at Saint Augustine College,[1] an American-Augustinian School in Havana. I was very fortunate to earn a four-year, fully paid scholarship at that school. After graduation, I enjoyed two years of working, without any worries other than learning my job, earning money, and having a good time with my friends.

My family went through what I think was a traumatic experience—my father and mother's divorce.

Then came the fateful day when a revolution took hold of an economically sound and fun-loving country with plenty of opportunities. I was much unprepared for such a drastic change in our country. Ultimately, I chose sides and slowly became involved in making political decisions, eventually finding myself in the middle of an armed invasion against Castro's Communist regime in Cuba.

The original synopsis of the Bay of Pigs Invasion that I wrote in 1964 would remain kept away somewhere, together with my other important documents, getting yellower and dustier. My oldest daughter, Tara, was the only one of my daughters who would show any interest in my account of the Bay of Pigs incident, maybe because it was a subject that came up when she was attending high school.

I shared with Tara the written account that I had put together. She laughed about my English syntax, grammatical errors, and misspellings (I knew about them); well, it had a lot to be desired, but the message was there. She suggested that perhaps I should write a book from the synopsis. I put that idea aside. I did not have the time, and when I did, I was not up to it. My jobs in the computer field kept me busy for many years; it just seemed that each company I worked for always had a project that needed to be completed as soon as possible, thus taking up much of my spare time.

When I retired, the idea of writing the book came up again. "Hey, Dad, maybe you'll have time for your book now." I was not mentally ready for this undertaking. I was still in a "working-on-a-job" mode. I thought that I was prematurely retired by my company, so I did not act on her suggestion; besides, rather than writing a book, I was supposed to develop my artistic skills and start drawing and painting again during my retirement years. I could not bring myself to get started on my drawing and painting, no matter how much prodding I got from one particular former coworker and friend, Maxine.

Out of nowhere, sometime in April 2006, I had the urge to try to write the book, so here it is. A long time has gone by, so using some of the details from my original synopsis and some serious memory searching, I started putting together a time line of events.

My story is very simple, and it is not only about the Bay of Pigs Invasion, although that is part of my life. I thought that, by relating my experiences while I was growing up, I could show my daughters, my grandchildren, or any young person who happened to read my book that I was not any different than they are. I relate how I dealt with my own disappointments, such as the loss of my first loves. While writing the book, I could see that, over my life, I changed someone who was only interested in banalities to someone who really cared about the important things in life; some of my coworkers and friends were very instrumental in making me realize that bigger things than my own little world existed—such as freedom.

My flimsy notes alone could not fill a book, so I started by interviewing and putting together memories from my good friends. The first person I contacted was my confidant and neighborhood friend Evelio; after all, he was the last person I was with before I left Cuba. I talked with my schoolmates from Saint Augustine College, Julio, Orlando, and Heriberto; my sisters, Zonia and Inez; my uncle Enrique's sons, Jorge and Enrique Jr.; my wife, Martha; and my father's sister, my favorite aunt, Salvadora. Also I gathered information from recently released documents, including the "CIA Historical Review Program Releases Sanitized 1997" under the Freedom of Information Act.

There are several good books about the Bay of Pigs Invasion out there. Many of them focus in detail not only on the logistics of the battle itself, but also on all of the political maneuvering during the Eisenhower and Kennedy administrations and the role of the CIA, the Department of Defense, and the National Security Agency; some of the books contain interviews and congressional hearings with some of the players at that time and include many details.

In this book, if I did not see it, live it, or hear it, it is not there. But I did provide, when needed and when I thought they were relevant to my story, actual CIA documents released under the Freedom of Information Act and, of course, my opinions from my political perspective.

I was not politically inclined during my teens, but I did understand the repercussions of living under a military dictatorship, like Batista's, or an ideological totalitarian dictatorship, such as Castro's brand of communism/ socialism. At that time, I was more concerned about graduating from school and having a good time and, once I'd graduated, on being able to find work and—did I say?—having a good time. Then along came Castro. I admit that, just like most everyone else, I got caught up, in the early days, in the swell of admiration and the possibility of change for the better— although no one realized what kind of change we were going to experience. As for me, I believe the honeymoon only lasted about five months.

As I said before, up until that point, my only concern and preoccupation as a young man was having a good time with my friends. Attending my Saturday nights dances at the Nautical Club, as well as my frequent visits to my favorite brothels—in my culture, it was not a big deal for a young man in his teens to visit a bordello. The last thing on my mind was to get political or, even more remote from my mind, commit an act of patriotism.

So when did I become politically aware? It all started when they took my Prostitutes away! How shallow can I possibly be? Wait; there is still hope for me! I began to realize that they had not only taken my Prostitutes away, but they were also taking property away from people who worked really hard for it and giving it to people who happened to be wearing a green uniform and a beard and had spent three months up in the mountains.

Businesses built by honest, hardworking, and enterprising people; enterprises that had provided jobs and livelihood to others—the Castro government began a systematic intervention (a new form of stealing) to take over these businesses. I was no longer thinking about having a good time; there were no good times to be had!

Freedom, as I knew it, was taken away by the government simply saying, "If you are not with the revolution, then you are the enemy of the revolution, and therefore, we will deal with you accordingly"—a direct threat to all Cuban citizens and their right of freedom of expression. I knew that it was time for me to go, but how? When?

I was able to leave Cuba with my uncle's help. My uncle Enrique provided me with the opportunity to become a merchant marine, just like him. (Chapter 9 goes into a great deal of detail on how this came about.) I thought that working as a merchant marine was the ideal situation for me; I would be away from the pressures of joining the system, at least for a while. And at the same time, I would be touching port back in Cuba, where I could see my family and friends and check out how things were going with the new regime. If the regime had not changed by then, I would jump off ship into another country, hopefully the United States, and ask for political asylum.

Life does not always go according to our plans; we touched port, for the first time, in New Orleans. I thought that this might be a good place for me to ask for political asylum. While in New Orleans, instead of seeking political asylum, I was given a choice. (Chapter 11 relates what I consider a drastic turning point in my life.) I had to choose between being a coward and being a patriot. From that point on, I was in the hands of God. Within a month of leaving Cuba, my very life was really going to be challenged in ways that I never, in a million years, would have envisioned.

Eventually it all worked out, as it always does, and I am a proud father of three beautiful daughters and three grandchildren.

Chapter 1

Crushes and Crashes

Mother's Day, May 12 1951, a beautiful Sunday morning, was still the dry season in Cuba; the early morning carried a nice, soft, cool breeze. The sky, which could be seen among a variety of architectural designs in buildings from different eras—from Spanish Colonial to Art Deco was blue with some puffy clouds here and there. After wishing my mother a happy Mother's Day and having breakfast with the family, I went out to our balcony. You could still smell the acridness of asphalt that had recently paved our street; by then, the city was in the process of completing the removal of the old 1920s vintage streetcar rails and converting to an all-bus mass transit system.

There was little traffic that morning; the narrow street was wide enough to fit a car and half, so the city had prohibited parking on that street due to it being a bus route. The same bunch of guys who always gathered at the corner grocery-bar diagonally across from my building—a typical pastime in Havana—were already there. I could see their hands moving with the rhythm of their conversation.

The jukebox at the Taberna de Pedro (Pedro's Tavern), a bar across from the grocery store had all doors open, ready for anybody to walk in. In old Havana, grocery stores, bar-groceries, and bars did not have any doors closed while they were open; they had no air-conditioning. (This same practice is in place at Sloppy Joe's in Key West.) Someone had already put a nickel in

1

the jukebox and played a Glenn Miller tune, "String of Pearls," as if Havana wanted to wake up nice and easy.

If my memory does not fail me, there was a Sloppy Joe's at the port of Havana. Sloppy Joe's bar and dining area was decorated with autographs of many famous Hollywood actors; Sloppy Joe's catered to the weekly visits from the cruise ships, mainly from Florida, as well as to sailors from the American Navy when they touched port. Sloppy Joe's was immediately closed by the Castro regime.

"Mom, I'm going to church; I have a mass to help with this morning, but I'll be back in about an hour," I said to my mother, after waiting a few minutes to see if Pilar Polon, the girl in the Art Deco building directly across from our building, was coming out onto her balcony. I lived on a second floor above a mezzanine of my building. Pilar was the only daughter of a Spaniard couple. Pilar had a nice, tan complexion; deep, dark eyes; dark hair a little straight that she kept about shoulder length; and a nice body, and I loved to look up her legs from my vantage point. Hey, I am a guy and I was only twelve, okay?

Back to my mother. "Your father wants you to go with him and help him out to mount a TV antenna at one of his customers' houses, so don't take too long," my mother said.

I stepped down the wide marble stairs at the ground floor. To my left was the spacious courtyard where the carriages of residents of times past, most likely Spaniard royalty, or, at the very least, the well-to-do were stored. The courtyard was surrounded by smaller apartments; during Spanish Colonial times, some of these apartments were originally used for storing horses and carriages supplies and housing for the drivers.

The mezzanine was for housing the servers of the mansion and the second and third floor, for the owner's family and visitors. The entrance door was huge, a door within the door. The entire door was to be opened only when the resident's carriages were coming in or out; the inner door opened for the people to get in and out. My apartment building covered a good portion of the street corner.

My walk to the church, Santo Cristo del Buen Viaje,[1] was not too far, about three and half blocks away. On my way to church, I passed a movie house called Cervantes. Across from Cervantes lived the cousins of another one of my crushes, or maybe my number-one crush, Emilia. Emilia lived in a three-story building with her parents, two brothers, and younger sister. The building was a little slender because each floor was a complete one-family apartment. I would see Emilia very often going by on her way to visit her cousins about a block and half from her residence. Just a few weeks before, I had started saying "hi" to her as she went by; I wanted to go really easy, making friends with her.

Santo Cristo Church, build circa 1510 and the "Santo Cristo" Parochial School at right. I officiated as altar boy for a couple of years.

After walking about two and half blocks, there it was—my grade school building. My family had managed to place me in a newly built Catholic parochial school, Santo Cristo Parochial School, founded by an American Augustinian priest, Father John McKniff, OSA.[2] The Augustinian Order[3] had instituted a program by which the two top honor students to graduate from the parochial school (grades one to six) were the recipients of a fully paid three-year scholarship at Saint Augustine School.[4] Saint Augustine was a private school established in 1901 and administered by an American Augustinian. The American Augustinians were also responsible for opening

Father John McKniff O.S.A. was relocated to the Augustinian missions in Peru, he is being considered for Sainthood.

the first private university in Latin America, Saint Thomas of Villanova University.

I was in the fifth grade at the time; for health reasons, I had lost about six months of my school schedule—my mother never told me exactly what those health reasons were, and I did not give the situation a lot of importance. My parochial school was next door to the church, and behind the church is Saint Augustine College, mentioned above. To the left of the church, there was a park. Sometimes, on the weekend, I would make a little money by helping at a wedding or a baptism, enough for me to go the movies, my second pastime, after girls. That day, I was just helping with Mass at 10:30 a.m. I had been an altar boy since the third grade, so I'd had a lot of experience by then. The priests were all American Augustinian; with just a few exceptions, they were all bilingual, and so at that time, for me, communicating with them was not a problem.

Main entrance to Saint Augustine College.

I liked the 10:30 a.m. Sunday Mass, although I was not always scheduled to help with it. Because, at that morning hour, a few American families attended Mass, the sermon was also given in English. I just loved to look at some of the girls my age that these families brought with them; they were just gorgeous. I was by myself that morning. It was a little extra work, but I did not mind.

When the time came to bless and distribute the sacrament, right in front of me was Emilia—my second love, with her dark blonde hair, light brown eyes, and friendly smile, she was just beautiful. (A couple of years later, I would find out that her older brother worked with my uncle Enrique on the SS *Florida*, a ship that sailed from Miami to Havana twice a week. A little leverage with Emilia? Maybe.) I was really nervous standing in front of her and holding the golden plate under her chin while the priest administered her the sacrament. I thought my soul was going to drain out of my feet, but I managed to keep my composure.

I had made some money the previous Saturday at church helping in a baptism, so I planned to go to the movies once I got back from helping my father. I thought his request for me to help him was a little strange; my father very rarely tried to bond with me. He was very quiet man—an introvert just like me. We both read tons of books. One of my favorite pastimes was drawing; my father also had the same talent. He was very diligent in making sure that I did my schoolwork; he was very demanding when it came to school matters. But we did not "hang out." Well, I thought that maybe he wanted to change the situation a little and wanted me to get involved in what he did.

My father finally had something going, after struggling toward the end of World War II, in the radio, appliance, and TV repair business, and although he graduated at the University of Barcelona with a degree in engineering and drafting, he was not practicing his career at this point.

On my way home from church, I bought a Mother's Day red flower to place on my shirt—a tradition in many Latin countries.

"Okay, are you ready to go?" my father asked me.

"Yes, where are we going?" I asked.

"Not far away. I need your help to secure a TV antenna on a roof for one of my clients; we'll be back in time for you to go to the movies, okay?"

"That's good," I answered.

My father and I stepped down the same marble stairs that I had gone down earlier. My father's first car, a light cream 1939 Ford V8 coupe—my uncle Enrique had a better car, a burgundy 1948 four-door Mercury—was parked at the street that intersected the bus route street, where it was okay to park, as long as you found a parking space.

There was one thing that I thought was a pain in the neck—you had to switch parking sides every other day; I never knew the logic behind that requirement. My father and I got in the car, he got the car started, and we were on our way. He reached the intersection. The old Havana streets did not have a lot traffics lights or stop signs, so beeping the horn at an intersection was a common way to let others know that you were coming.

Everything happened so quickly. Within a few seconds, I heard a crashing noise; I felt a warm liquid oozing and running down my face, dripping onto the pieces of broken glass sitting on my lap; the liquid was red. There were no seatbelts in a 1939 Ford. I was in a daze, not knowing what had really happened to me. Someone opened the door on my side and took me out. My vision was a little blurred, but I actually felt no pain.

I do recall someone stopping a taxicab, which just happened to go by. Somehow, the person who helped me out of the car got a towel and placed it on my face to help me contain the bleeding. Later on, after I had recovered, I would find out that the man who opened the car door and helped me out worked at the Cervantes movie theater; he knew me from going to the movies almost every Sunday. He, my father, and I rode in the backseat of the taxi to the closest local emergency facility.

"Are you hurt?" the man from the theater helping us asked my father.

"No, I'm okay; just my belt buckle is bent," my father responded.

Apparently, he hit the steering wheel at the waist level; I am sure that he had to have been black and blue on his stomach for a while.

At the emergency facility, the medics moved me out to a room right away. I was lying down on a table, bleeding like a pig, and the medical staff started to assist me. I was still sort of dazed, but I remember hearing one of the attending physicians exclaim, "We have to clean the wound and check to see if there are any small pieces of glass embedded."

"This is going to hurt, kid," he said.

I felt a cold liquid running down my face. It smelled like alcohol, and it burned, but I could not scream.

"Let's start the sutures," I heard another attending nurse or physician saying.

Now I was really hurting—all thirty-six stitches worth.

I returned home from the emergency facility. My face was all covered in bandages, and my parents brought me to my bed. I was still a little groggy. Everything happened so fast that the full impact of what happened to me had not totally reached my brain yet. My sister Inez was just looking at me. My face did feels very stiff, and I really couldn't talk. My mother was expecting my future sister Zonia. Some of my neighbors came to see me and were standing by my bed talking and asking questions. Of course I couldn't talk. Somehow, I felt embarrassed. I was so tired; I fell asleep.

A couple of days later, my father sat next to me and related what really had happened. A woman had left the sidewalk and begun crossing the street at the same time that my father started turning. She was carrying a grocery bag on her arms, but at the time, my father thought that she was carrying a baby in her arms. He got so nervous that he stepped on the gas pedal instead of the brake; at the same time, he started to turn away from the woman but lost control of the car—no power steering on a 1939

Ford. He came to a full stop against a wall opposite from the grocery-bar establishment not too far away from the movie cinema. I could tell that my father felt very guilty about the accident and that it was me, and not him, who had been hurt. He apologized to me. I told him not to worry and that it was just an accident.

I asked my mother to move my bed to the living room, next to the huge French doors leading to our balcony. I hated being in a darker room, without sunlight. Besides I could now look up at Pilar Polon's legs again. About a month after recovering from my accident, I asked Pilar to ask her parents if they would allow me to visit her. To my surprise, they said yes. I visited her several times, until my crush on Emilia got too intense.

During my stay at home, my fifth-grade teacher—who, by the way, was very young and a good looker—came to see me and brought homework for me so that I would not fall behind with my studies. I was embarrassed because, just a few weeks before my accident, my mother had been called to school by the principal about my behavior. I do not know how it came about; maybe it was an age thing—a stage I fell into—but I started to say everything with a double meaning, a lot of it with sexual connotations. I was called to the principal's office with my mother present. Fortunately, my mother gave me a break, and she did not tell my father about this incident. Otherwise, I would not have had the opportunity of writing this book. Very embarrassing. I apologized to my teacher and my mother again for my past behavior.

It seemed to me that my bandages were on for a long time, but I think it was for about ten days. My mother took me to the same emergency facility where I'd been taken care of on the day of the accident to have my stitches removed.

"Whoever did your stitching did a very good job," said the nurse while he was removing my stitches. I was on pins and needles during the whole procedure.

"They healed really nice; in a couple of years, when you get older, you won't even know they are there," said the male nurse as he applied a piece of cotton saturated with alcohol to clean out the scabs.

"That's easy for you to say; it didn't happen to you," I finally managed to say once he finished his job. We went home; I did not want to see a mirror anywhere near me.

The following Monday, I would start school again. I wasn't sure I could handle it, so I had to look at myself in the mirror and deal with it.

We did not have a big mirror in the bathroom, so it was easy for me to avoid it. I closed the door behind me and closed my eyes. I started feeling the wall in the area where the mirror was. I found it. I slowly opened my eyes, and there they were—three scars.

The scars were still red; you could see the little holes where the sutures had been made. The largest one was on my left cheek and started just millimeters from my eyeball; it looked like an inverted letter L. The next one was about half an inch long on an angle at the tip of my right brow crossing and ending right over my eyelid. The glass had stopped cutting my eyelid just a millimeter from the top of my eyeball—I can still feel a little indent on my eye socket bone. The last one was under my lower lip. *No girl is going to want me, looking like this!* I said to myself.

Here is what I had to deal with. I was very skinny, flesh and bones only—my nickname at school was "El Flaco" (skinny one). I had great hair and eyes; that was it.

My mother took me to several pediatricians to see if they could do something for me. "Is anyone in your family or his father's family fat?" All the doctors would ask my mother the same question. "No, nobody," my mother would always answer. It did not matter how much I ate, how often I ate, or what kind of food I ate; nothing happened. And now I was marked for life. I was doomed.

My first day at school after the car accident, I had to repeat my story about the accident many times. I honestly was very surprised that so many

My first love, Elena Czieska in the third grade at the Parochial School, I was in the fourth grade.

guys in my school knew me because I was very quiet and an introvert for the most part. I only had one or two close friends. My troubles were not over yet, oh no. About a month before my accident, I had become—ta da da da—a *stalker*!

Ever since the fourth grade, my eyes had noticed Elena Siezcka, a beautiful, blonde, blue-eyed Polish girl. I just loved that girl. I used to follow her home. Whenever possible, my face was in front of her, trying to make eye contact with her. I could not say anything to her other than "hi."

Just a few days after coming back to school, I was called to the principal's office. Miss Imelda, the principal, and Elena's teacher, Margarita, were there too.

"We have a problem here, Desiderio. Elena has complained to us about you; she says that you have been following her home, and it seems that you are everywhere. What do you have to say about this?" the principal said with a stern look on her face.

"Well, it's true, but I didn't mean any harm by it. I just ... love her," I answered, embarrassed that my long-held secret has been uncovered.

"You're making her feel very, very uncomfortable, and she maybe even feels scared. Is that what you want?" Imelda said, looking into my eyes very intensely.

"Well ... no," I answered.

"We are not going to do anything to you right now, but you have to promise us that you are going to stop this; otherwise, we may be force to suspend you or even worse expel you from school. Do you understand?" Imelda said forcefully.

"You have my word that I'm not going to do it anymore." *Oh, God my life is now over.*

The next month was going to be June, graduation from the fifth grade. I decided I was going to behave myself; I set the goal of being the winner of one of the full scholarship available for the recipients of the two highest grades for Saint Augustine. I spend that summer reading my favorite books, *The Shadow*, *Doc Savage*, cowboy novels by Zane Gray, and others. I also did a lot of drawing, working on my stamp collections, and building model airplanes. But I had not given up on Emilia yet.

During the school year of 1952–1953, I started to get more involved in parochial affairs, along with officiating as an altar boy almost every morning for early Mass. I was also getting involved with Father McKniff and his Catholic youth organizations, as well as the Boy Scouts. I was keeping very busy, just to get my mind off Elena Siezcka and be true to my promise.

Lucky me, I was walking toward school one Saturday morning, walking past the Cervantes movie house. I stopped to look at the bill for Sunday and I heard, "Pssst, pssst; look up here."

Oh, my God, Emilia's cousins are calling me.

"Who me?" I said as I looked up.

Who else could it be? I am the only one around, I said to myself.

"Come up for a minute, okay."

I went up. The two sisters were at the top of the one flight of stairs, the door was opened, and they were smiling. *These girls are just gorgeous,* I said to myself. They were a couple of years older than I was.

"I am Susana, and my sister's name is Vanesa. Come here; sit down a minute."

"What is your name?" Susana asked me, smiling.

"Desiderio." I could not get over my shock.

"Oh, just like your father's name," Vanesa said.

"You know my father?" I was taken aback. "How … When?"

"He was here fixing our radio and TV console just a few weeks ago," Vanesa said.

"Yeah … and we recognized him from the accident down the street a few months ago, so we asked him about you," Susana added.

"Oh," I exclaimed. I had not known that. Of course, my father never told me about it, not that he shared many things with me.

"So you are the boy who got hurt in the car accident? Can we look at the scars? How did it feel? Did it hurt a lot?"

They were both asking me questions, taking turns.

"Well, yeah …" I spend about half an hour talking to them about the accident.

"Well, I think I better go." I got from the sofa, and as I started taking my first steps downstairs, I then turned around and said, "Do you mind if I ask you a question?"

"No, ask us," they responded.

"Are you related to Emilia? I see her coming down this way a lot." I knew they were related, but I pretended as if I did not know. I wanted to make sure that Emilia's cousins did not think that I had ulterior motives to befriend them.

"Yeah, she's our cousin," they both responded.

Oh boy, oh boy! I thought with rejoice.

As I was leaving, they said something else to me. "Desiderio, we want you to come and visit us anytime, okay? We mean it."

Their response was totally unexpected, and I felt very good about it. I thought that befriending Emilia's cousins was a great opportunity for me, and added a different dimension to my quest to conquer Emilia. Something else occurred to me; having my face scarred had not really hurt me as I'd thought it would. My fears of rejection had not materialized at all. If nothing else, I thought, it had helped me—to be different, to be noticed, to sort of stand out from the crowd.

I visited with Emilia's cousins often; sometimes Emilia was there visiting them as well. We talked about, you know, movies, music, friends, but I could not bring myself to tell Emilia how I felt about her. I did not think that I would feel too good about being rejected. I think eventually I did tell her cousins about my feelings for her, but that did not help at all. I did not push the issue; maybe time would help.

She invited me to her *quinceañera* (the Latin version of a sweet sixteen party, except it celebrates a girls fifteenth birthday). I danced with her a few times; I wished it had been all the time with her, but she was the host, so she danced with all her friends.

June 1953 arrived, and it was time to graduate from the sixth grade. I had made it. I had reached my goal. I was one of the top students graduating from the parochial school. In September, I was going to start at Saint Augustine with a fully paid scholarship. I had a lot of work to do between June and September.

Ninety percent of the school topics at Saint Augustine were taught in English. I knew very little English, practically nothing; it was cramming time now! I was able to get help from the new principal of the school, Father Kennedy. I already knew Father Kennedy from serving as his altar boy several times. I told him my concern about learning English with so little time available between now and next September; he said he would help me.

Father Kennedy went out of his way to prepare for me a very condensed, high impact English grammar book; the booklet was typed and bound in a folder. "Study this book. Listen to English as much as you can. American music would be good. Try to read newspapers and magazines, even if don't understand any of it. Work with a dictionary at hand, and learn as many words as you can. You will be ready."

The first six months, from September 1953 to February 1954, were very stressful for me as far as school was concerned. I worked very hard at learning enough English to be able to follow business math, accounting, English literature, and other topics.

My efforts paid off. By the time I completed my first year at Saint Augustine, I was able to handle my academic load. Failure was not an option; one of the premises of the scholarship was that I could not repeat a grade.

During the year from 1953 to 1954, just to keep, the "edge" off, I listened to lots of American music on Radio Kramer in my room. I listened to Radio Kramer every day. The station played a good variety of music—big bands, rock 'n' roll, pop, and other varieties—during the days and evenings.

My favorite radio show was *The Hit Parade*. *The Hit Parade* was broadcasted on Saturday evenings about 7:30 p.m. It kept me current with the top American songs and artists of the week; my all-time favorite artist was Bill Haley and the Comets. He was followed by Elvis, Sammy Davis Jr., Frank Sinatra, the Platters, Nat King Cole, and many others.

My father had built me a very simple, one-transistor radio. He had some extra high fidelity earphones that provided excellent sound; I listened to my music there. The radio did not require any electricity or batteries. I could not understand why it worked all the time. It just picked up stations' signals through an antenna. Maybe I should point out that my father was also a radio ham. By then, he had built his second radio station transmitter/receiver, of about 5,000 watts of power. He had exchanged ham radio calling cards with other ham operators worldwide. His radio antenna was mounted on the rooftop of our apartment building, about forty feet high. My one-transistor radio was connected to that antenna.

My other stress reliever and outlet was a stamp collection that my father had started while at the university in Barcelona back in the late 1920s. The collection comprised of worldwide stamps. By the time he gave it to me, it was already very valuable I added a substantial amount of valuable stamps to the collection as well. In 1953, I purchased a stamp catalogue, and I valued the collection at that time at about $148,000. Another one of my hobbies was building model airplanes out of balsa wood, very intricate and time consuming, but very rewarding; none of the glue-together, plastic, assemble-in-two-hours models of today. Those airplanes took days to complete.

My school building's portals led into a vestibule. To the left, it led to my schoolrooms and stairs; the right led to the church sacristy. This portal became the meeting place for me and many of my friends. Among the guys I met during my early days at Saint Augustine was Alfredo Cruz, nicknamed "El Chino" (the Chinese). Alfredo was about my height. He had dark blond hair; his legs were somewhat short when compared with the rest of his body; and, according to everyone who knew him well, he was a terrific dancer.

Alfredo was also a handful, as far as behavior was concerned; he would eventually be expelled from Saint Augustine, by the time I reached my second year there.

I thought, *What a terrific idea.* I would learn how to dance. I could hold a girl real close legally, without getting in trouble. I asked Alfredo to teach me dancing. He did, and I have been dancing ever since.

Is the summer of 1955, around mid-August, I was enjoying my school vacation, after having completing my first year at Saint Augustine. I had continued following, to the letter, the admonition Father Kennedy had given me two years earlier and was immersing myself in the English language. Diagonally across from my former parochial school was another grocery-bar combination. The establishment had a jukebox, and I had several five-cent coins in my pocket. I invested all of these coins playing my old-time favorite rock 'n' roll song—Bill Haley's "Rock around the Clock":

One, two, three o'clock
Four o'clock, rock.
...

Ever since I'd seen the movie *Black Board Jungle* a few days before, that was all I wanted to hear; I had memorized the words of the song. The bar's jukebox across my apartment building did not have that song in it. The bartender had already asked me if there was another song I may want to play. Just to oblige to him, I played "Thirteen Women":

Last night I was dreaming
Dreamed about the H-Bomb ...

Side B of "Rock around the Clock," a very long song for that era.

I was totally fascinated with "Rock around the Clock," which is my number-one song even today.

That same summer of 1955, I made friends with Leandro Rodriguez. Leandro was about my height and had curly blond hair and little, round shoulders. I think he was a year ahead of me in school, but we connected through the American music. Independently from one another, we learned and sang in duo to the lyrics of a Frank Sinatra song that was number one in the hit parade at that time, "Learning the Blues":

The tables are empty; the dance floor's deserted.
They play the same love song; it's the tenth time you heard it ...

I do not know what Leandro's reason was for learning that particular song, but for me, I can pretty much guess what my motivation was.

Leandro and I got together quite often, usually on Saturday mornings. My routine was to walk to my school portal behind the church and wait to see which of my friends would show up. Leandro was there often; we just talked about American movies or the most current songs from Frank Sinatra and Sammy Davis Jr., our other favorite American singer.

Leandro's father was an excellent tailor. I was getting a little tired of the outfit that my grandfather had bought me when I turned fifteen— blue pants, a light pearl white sport jacket, a white shirt, and blue tie. I convinced Leandro to talk to his dad and see about him making me a sport jacket. His dad tailored me a beautiful black velvet sport jacket, and I bought a light blue, silk shirt and grey pants to go with it. I think I looked like a million dollars. I remember paying just forty dollars for each of the jackets he tailored for me—what a bargain!

Ever since Alfredo (el Chino) had taught me how to dance, I'd frequented the Galician and Austrian community centers in old Havana. These centers had open dances every Saturday night, and with my new "hot" outfit, I no longer felt embarrassed about wearing the same set of clothes every time.

Another piece of Americana that impressed me as a teenager was the 1955 James Dean's film *Rebel without a Cause*. I really could not understand why a bunch of high schoolers with a car of their own would have any problems. Of course, I was still trying to understand the American culture. But still, at that time, I was somehow able to identify with James Dean's character, and I became a James Dean fan. I was very saddened when he met his demise so early in life.

I had stayed away as much as possible from thinking about any of my crushes. I did not see Elena Czieska ever again but would come to find out that her older brother, Eduardo, was attending Saint Augustine; he was a couple of years ahead of me.

I did not visit with Emilia much during my first year at Saint Augustine; I did see her from my balcony, as she went by my apartment building to visit her cousins.

Other times I used to meet my neighborhood friend Armando Adam. Armando was about my height; he had short cut, black hair and a good build—he wasn't skinny like me. He was going to a military academy, and he wore his uniform after school, which was very attractive to many of the girls. Many afternoons, after school and before supper, we would stand at the corner bar chatting and watching the girls go by. Just a block away, in the direction of my school, there was a lower priced bordello. I used to go by sometimes on my way to a store, and the women would call me in as I went by. But I was not into that yet and wouldn't even consider going in; I was still too young.

The following year, in 1956, the Four Lads had a hit record named for exactly what we did:

Standing on the corner watching all the girls go by
Brother you don't know a nicer occupation ...

Just thinking about it takes me back to that time.

Sometimes Emilia would go by on her way to visit her cousins in the afternoon. We would just wave to her and say hi; she was always walking on the opposite side of the street, the same side of the street where her cousins lived. As she got older, she looked prettier, and of course, she was developing very nicely as well. I always found it irritating when the men standing at the corner of the grocery-bar would whisper "flatteries" at her as she went by—I never approved of the custom among Latin men to tell flatteries, sometimes bordering on the obscene, to women as they went by.

I think it happened one Saturday morning as I walking toward the Santo Cristo Plaza—as it was known at that time, where the park, the church and my school building were all located—to meet my friends. I stopped over at Emilia's cousin's home. We were just talking, and then Emilia came up the stairs. As usual, I got that funny feeling in the stomach. I do not know if what happened next was planned by Emilia's cousins; of course they knew about my feelings for Emilia. Her cousins just disappeared, and Emilia and I were left alone. I do not recall the exact conversation, but I think we started talking about parties, music, and such. Her cousins also listen to Radio Kramer, so the radio was on, and a song from Nat King Cole started playing:

Unforgettable, that's what you are
Unforgettable, though near or far ...

I do not know where I got the courage from, but I asked her to dance. She felt so good in my arms; I know I was a little shaken, but I managed to hide it. That was the only time, other than on her birthday party, that I was able to hold Emilia close to me. Her light perfume enhanced my experience. We danced the entire song very slowly and very closely. I could not believe it. We did not say a word, and this time was really special to me because it was just her and me. I was never going to see another chance like this one, ever! Why in the hell did I not say anything—*smack!* *Smack!* You idiot! I had a problem when it came to Emilia; I felt totally inadequate for her, and I thought she was way out of my league. I was absolutely sure that she would reject me.

Many days went by after my brilliant performance at Emilia's cousins. I had no choice than to go by their apartment building since I lived just a quarter of a block away, between Emilia's cousins' apartment building and Emilia's apartment building. One of those times, on my way home from school, one of her cousins called me from their balcony and asked me why I was not visiting them as often anymore. I went upstairs and I told them that I was very busy at school, but I would come back as soon as I could to visit them. Very soon, seeing or visiting Emilia or her cousins was to become a more difficult task for me.

Toward the end of 1955, my father decided to close his appliance and TV repair business and got a job in Lamas Industrial Laundry Service, located in Luyano Township, maintaining the company's industrial equipment. It was better for him because it related to what he was trained for; he was even able to buy a light green 1950 Studebaker, very different from the 1939 Ford.

His new job meant that our family had to move from downtown Havana to the suburbs. He chose Santo Suarez-La Vibora suburbs, about twenty-five minutes from downtown Havana by bus and closer to my father's new job. I became a daily commuter. Public transportation in Havana and its suburbs was excellent. To go to school, I had to take a bus, Route 14; the bus stop was right outside my apartment building in La Vibora. The bus would me let off at a park right across the street from Saint Augustine school in Old Havana, a trip of about forty minutes.

Fortunately, for me, two of my schoolmates, Oscar Sanchez and Pedro Roque also lived in La Vibora, so it made my trip to and from school much more enjoyable and made the bus trip go by much faster.

I made new neighborhood friends—Rodi Betancourt, Lazaro Leon, and Evelio Suao. I also became a member of the Columbian Squires, and organization I would be involved in for several years. Columbian Squires[5] was a youth organization under the direction of the Knights of Columbus, of which I had the charge of being the notary (secretary).

I occasionally went back to my old neighborhood in old Havana for the purpose of seeing Emilia again. I visited her cousins a couple of times, but without having a phone, it was hard for me to coordinate my visits. I had to face reality—my days of attempting to win Emilia's heart were coming to an end.

Chapter 2

Rock 'n' Roll, Bullets, Graduation, and Girls

Rock 'n' roll was becoming the culture among my friends and school buddies; since 1956, Elvis Presley and his music was becoming known by many around the world, and we could not get enough of this music. We decided to form a little group and wear a uniform. We bought the same shirt; it had vertical lines about half an inch wide alternating with yellow, black, and white; we all wore black pants; and someone in our group got a hold of hats with a picture of Elvis Presley in his famous "Heartbreak Hotel" stance. Our group consisted of Oscar, Julio, Pedro, Orlando, Evelio, Juan, and me.

Our group went together to the movies, all dressed alike. Of course, we are just teens, and we were just having fun. Our neighborhood movie theater, Los Angeles, was showing a new rock and roll movie named *Rock around the Clock*; of course I was going to see it. The movie itself did not have a great plot, but who cared? It was all rock and roll. The movie had performances by The Platters—who had sold over two million of their records—Little Richard, Fats Domino, Alan Freed, Freddie Bell, Tony Martinez, and last but not least, Bill Haley and his Comets; Bill Haley had sold twenty-five million of his records.

The movie theater was packed; we were all singing along with the music and screaming. Then, sometime during a dialogue in the movie, Juan Carajaville, one of my schoolmates, made a comment. "If somebody places a bomb in this theater ..."

Within a few minutes, some men sitting right behind us told us that we had to leave and go to the lobby of the theater. There at the lobby waiting for us were the same two men; they identified themselves as members of the Servicio de Inteligencia Militar (Military Intelligence Service).

We were all now being interrogated—where did we live? What were our names? What was the name of our school? Where was the bomb? Why were we all dressed alike? We told them that Juan had made a bad joke, we went to an American School, and we had no reason to do anything like that. After questioning us for a while, the men believed us but said we had to leave and could not come back into the theater. Thank you, Juan.

During 1956 and through 1958, my friends and I were frequent visitors at Elba's home. My friends, Elba, with her black, curly, not quite shoulder-length hair; her slightly round face; her full lips and dark brown, long-lashed, smiley eyes; her medium tan skin complexion; and her five foot four, well-proportioned, and very shapely body, seemed very happy all the time.

Evelio, who stood about five six, had wavy, dark blond hair that he kept short, a light tan skin complexion; and a muscular body, though not the body of a person who is working out all the time, and he wasn't even thinking of shaving yet. Evelio was the youngest guy in my group of friends.

When I met Evelio, he was still attending high school; he was very smart and blended well with the guys in our group. Lazaro (aka Lasi) was about six two with a very slender build. He was dark skinned, with thick, black hair that was just a little long and very straight and a pleasant, high cheek-boned face that he did not need to shave often. I think he was about my age. Lasi often had severe bouts with migraine headaches. We lived in the same apartment building, but he lived on the first floor, and I lived on the third floor. Lasi, sometimes, would stay in his room without coming out for two or three days, reading and smoking.

Cuban parents are very old-fashioned and very protective of their children, especially girls. But Elba's father, Matias, was a cool guy. He was the proud owner of a 1956 red and white Buick convertible[1] and was one of the owners of a lumber company. Whenever we visited his home, he talked to us and received us openly. Elba was our friend; there was nothing romantic going on. We were just good friends having good times together. My friendship with Elba and her family would turn out to be advantageous for me in the not-too-distant future.

And then, I met Maida Donate, a beautiful girl who stood about five foot five and had short, black hair; dark brown eyes; full lips; and dark skin. She was attending an all girls' school not to far away from my apartment building in La Vibora; she gave me a couple of her pictures with a dedication written on the back.

There was one thing I was not able to totally understand—why was she going to that school when her parents owned a school, Donate Institute, on a second floor located about two and half miles from my building? Right across the way from her parents' school and residence was a central bus stop, where transfers were made to many other routes that would take commuters to El Vedado, downtown Havana, and many other locations.

My third love, Maida Donate, circa 1956, at school. I had moved out of Habana by then, and lost contact with my second love; Emilia.

I am not sure how I connected with Maida, but it had to have been while her school bus would stop by my building waiting for the traffic light to change. Maybe our eyes met while I was standing and talking to my friends, and I just took the chance to talk to her. I probably told her that I liked her very much. I am sure that she said likewise; that is how I got her picture.

Cuban parents did not make it easy for guys to go from a platonic relationship to something more serious; it meant that I had to actually take the daring step of going to Maida's home, knocking on the door, and telling her parents that I wanted to visit their daughter. She was younger than I was; I thought that I would just get her in trouble. I did not do anything. I think that, under normal circumstances, she would have replaced my humungous crush with Emelia.

Destiny had other plans reserved for me—1957 started with a series of happenings that were precursors of ominous and deep changes in the culture and political spectrum of my country. These changes would have a lasting impact on many generations of Cubans.

Finally, June 1957 rolled around, and I was graduating from Saint Augustine and starting my future in real life. I never paid that much attention to politics—nobody ever does when a teenager—but the adults around me were saying that the political situation in Cuba was deteriorating. President Batista, through a *coup d'état* on March 10, 1952, took over the government and promised eventual national elections.

About four or five years into his government, and about the time that general elections would have been scheduled, Batista decided to remain in government as a dictator. Soon after that, a declaration from Batista, suspending constitutional guarantees under the Cuban constitution, was broadcasted by radio and TV; no more elections would be forthcoming.

Over the next several years, after Batista declaring himself president for life, or at least made it clear that he would not be stepping down in a foreseeable future, national unrest set in; repression by the Batista regime was getting more and more severe. A group of rebels commanded by a young lawyer named Fidel Castro took to the mountains in Santiago, after attacking a military quarters in a western province. Castro and other and anti-Batista groups began to gain political ground and expand their influence.

Although the Batista government had intelligence and publicly published documents that proved that the main rebel group, the 26th of July Movement, headed by Castro and his brother, Raul, was Communist inspired, no one believed the government at that time. The media of the time did not put sufficient emphasis on this point to alert the people about Castro's leanings. That same media, which basically promoted him, was decimated (well deservedly) by the Castro regime once he consolidated his power.

A group of idealistic University of Havana students formed an anti-Batista militant group, comprised of members of the Havana University Student Federation and members of the armed wing of the Cuban Republican Party. A student named Jose Antonio Echevarria headed this group called Directorio Revolucionario; the group was renamed Directorio Revolucionario 13 de Marzo (Revolutionary Directory March 13) after the Presidential Palace attack. Echevarria, together with a group of forty-two students, planned and coordinated an attack on the Presidential Palace, as well as the takeover of a radio station located in the CMQ-La Rampa complex. The attack took place on March 13, 1957, with the purpose of condemning and promoting the removal of the regime, as well as to inspire the citizens to rebel against the Batista government. The group was trying to force the resignation of Batista and prevent a takeover by Castro's movement.

The day of the attack on the Presidential Palace, I was at school, and the time was about 3:00 p.m. Our school hours were from 8:00 a.m. to 4:00 p.m. About three school buses serviced those children who lived outside of the parish and were able to afford the transportation fee.

At about 3:30 p.m., the school principal sounded the alarm. Of course, we did not know exactly what was going on at the time, though we heard all kinds of rumors. Parents of the children who lived nearby came to the school right away to pick up their children. We found out from several of the parents that a shootout between a group that had taken over the Museo de Bellas Artes (Art Museum) building and the Presidential Palace military guards was underway.

The attack by the organized students went down as follows: The group of forty-two students had split into two groups. A group of thirty-four commenced its attack on the palace, and the other group of eight, simultaneously, was to occupy Radio Reloj (Clock Radio), located at La Rampa complex, on 23rd Avenue and L Street. The purpose of the radio station takeover was to inform the people about the attack on the Presidential Palace and its purpose.

Across from the Art Museum and between the two buildings, a well-maintained park, with a garden of well-trimmed bushes and flowers of contrasting color, benches provided a resting place for pedestrians. Across from the park, exactly at the Presidential Palace's main entrance, was a bus stop for several routes, among them, my route.

When the shooting started, a bus was already at the stop letting off and picking up passengers. Although the bus driver was wounded in the shooting, he was able to drive a few yards away in an attempt to get his passengers out of harm's way. He died at the wheel a few moments later; many of the passengers in the bus had also been killed in the crossfire.

After the shooting was over, twenty-two of the students lay dead. The other twelve made their escape but where later captured, in a "safe" house.

The other group of eight, headed by Echevarria, was still holding out at the radio station and was able to read and transmit the group's message. Radio Reloj was located in the fourth floor of the La Rampa CMQ-Building. On his way out of the building, Echevarria shot and wounded a police officer guarding the main entrance of the building. He then made his escape by foot, walking down on 23rd Avenue toward the Havana University complex.

Echevarria was already walking by the university when he saw a police patrol car coming up in his direction. Thinking that he had been spotted and that the officers were coming after him, he took out his gun and started firing at the police. The police responded to the fire directed at them, and Echevarria received several shots and died at the very steps of his university. After it was all over, the police officers involved in the shooting asked, "Who is this guy?" The police did not know at that time that they had killed Jose Antonio Echevarria. Had Echevarria survived his efforts, according to people very close to him, he eventually would have been executed by Castro for being antirevolutionary.

The remainder of the group in the radio station was apprehended and jailed. Eventually, one of planners of the coordinated attack on the Presidential Palace and Radio Reloj, Faure Chomon, founded the Directorio Revolucionario 13 de Marzo, named after the day Echevarria died. The M-13-DR groups took to the Escambray Mountains, two provinces west of Havana Province, and had the distinction of being the first rebel group marching full force into Havana.

Meanwhile, at Saint Augustine College, those of us who took city transportation, for safety reasons, were kept at the school building until about 6:30 p.m. On our way home, as expected, all traffic near the area of the Presidential Palace had been diverted from its usual route.

I was saddened to learn from the conductor[2] and the driver of another Route 14 bus that took me home that evening some of the details of the shootings during the Presidential Palace attack. My school friends and I knew most of the drivers and conductors. The bus driven by the ill-fated driver had just stopped at the bus stop at the Presidential Palace to pick up and let off passengers; at that precise moment, the shooting started, and he and his bus were caught in the crossfire. The driver, even though he was mortally wounded, was able to drive a little farther away from the line of fire, and then he died. Unfortunately, the conductor and several of the passengers had been killed by then. All I knew at that moment was that my friends and I had just missed that bus, by less than an hour.

My graduation from Saint Augustine College was held in June 1957. Saint Augustine graduations were held at the Galician Center, not far from my school.

The Galician Center was a beautiful Gothic building near the capitol building that was built by the Spaniards. The inside was mostly white marble; it was very spacious, with wide marble stairs, high ceilings, and large windows. The center was not air-conditioned, but it always felt very cool inside, no matter the temperature outside. During the weekend, the center had dances with a different orchestra on each of the three floors; you could find me there on most Saturday nights.

Unfortunately, my school graduation did not go as I expected. Due to threats and rumors of bombings by anti-Batista organizations, our graduation could not be held at the Galician Center; our safety could not be guaranteed. My graduation was held inside the Santo Cristo Del Buen Viaje Church. It was the first time since the inception of the college that a graduation had been held inside the church. I was very disappointed, especially because photos were not allowed inside the church.

A few weeks after my graduation, my friends and I were visiting Elba's home. Elba, Lasi, Evelio, and I were hanging out in her living room listening to records of our favorite American singers—even after all the significant events going on around me, I was still oblivious as to what was to come and how my country would be transformed beyond recognition. Our conversation gravitated to our favorite topics.

"So, did you know that Elvis's 'Teddy Bear' has now been number one on *Billboard* and on Radio Kramer for seven weeks?" said Evelio, always well informed.

"Yeah, I like that song a lot. Isn't there an Elvis movie where he sings that song?" Elba responded, smiling.

"I don't know for sure," I said, adding, "I also like 'All Shook Up' a lot; it's a good dancing song. I think that song was on top of the charts for eight weeks."

"Do you like Pat Boone?" Lasi asked. "He does have a nice song in 'Love Letters in the Sand.'" Lasi did not know a lot about American music, but he tried, and it was a nice song; I'll give him credit.

He never received an answer.

"Well, now that you mentioned sand, school is out. I'll be able to go to the beach and the movies more often," Elba said, sounding very happy.

"Did any of you guys see *The Bridge on the River Kwai* yet?" Evelio asked, trying to continue with the movies topic.

"Yeah I did," I told him, adding, "That movie is based on a true story! And it's very good."

"Not me," said Elba firmly. "I like romantic movies better, something like … last year's *Anastasia*."

"Talking about school, I better put more time and effort into looking for a job now that I graduated," I said, even though it had been awhile since "the school word" had been mentioned. I think that, without realizing it, I was doing a little bit of networking.

"Oh, yeah, you know, I think my dad is looking for someone to help him at the office at the Lumber Company. Do you want me to talk to him about it for you when he comes back from work?" Elba said pointing and waving her finger at me.

I opened my eyes in a gesture of surprise and immediately responded, "Yeah, I'm interested. I am definitely interested; please talk to your dad."

"Did you guys hear that new song on Radio Kramer? I think it goes ... 'Great Balls of Fire.' It's from a new singer named Jerry ... something," Lasi said, trying to get back to the original music topic.

***

A couple of days later, I had an interview with Matias. Matias was about five foot five and slightly potbellied. His wavy hair was still black, with a few scattered gray hairs, but balding in some spots. He had a semiotic nose and wore black-rimmed glasses. His skin tone was a little darker than his daughters. He was a very talkative person and friendly, but capable of being strong when rebuking or showing his authority.

I entered the office where he works. It was an open office, with about three desks and a lot of activity. Because the cash register was on a desk in front of his, there was a lot of in-and-out activity from customers and sales people alike. He still managed to interview me.

"Come in. Have a seat. My daughter talked to me about you, and she told me that you are interested in working here. So ... Desi, tell me what did you graduate in?" Matias was seated across from me, and he looked straight at my eyes as he asked.

"Well, my college majors were accounting, business math, and general office management, English, and algebra," I answered, a little nervous but maintaining eye contact. "It is an equivalent of an associate's degree in Business Administration. I graduated at the top of my class, even though in the beginning I had a little trouble with algebra," I continued explaining; I wanted to be honest with him.

"Okay, that is good. I am going have you start to work as a cashier first. You can also help us collect from our customers who buy on credit, and you can help Ariel in the yard when things get a little slow, learn a little about the lumber business," Matias responded. He did not seem too concerned about algebra.

"That sounds really good; I know I will be good at this job. I'd like to learn about this business. I really appreciate this opportunity, Mr. Ferrero," I said, breathing much easier.

"Just call me Matias, okay?" he responded.

"Okay so ... when do I start?" I asked.

I accepted his offer since the job sounded like a good place for me to start. I had just graduated and had not expended a great deal of time in searching for a job.

The lumber company was undergoing a great time of growth. The company sold imported woods from Central and South America, as well as native woods and had started expanding to Formica, plywood, and pressed woods. Many of the customers were furniture stores, independent custom furniture makers, and carpenters. I worked there for about two years. At that point, I wanted to try something new and to begin to expand my working experience, so I went to work for a liquor distributor until the revolution took over. I left that job a couple of weeks after January 1, 1959.

Lumber Company luncheon, circa 1958. From left to right; Eduardo, Julio, Osvaldo, Ariel (one of the partners,) Eduardo, Martin (one of the partners,) Desi and Matias (one of the partners.)

My social life during the months and the year following my graduation from Saint Augustine College, 1957 and 1958, was what I considered pretty normal. I liked my job at the lumber company, got together often with my friends, and frequented nightclubs, and of course, I fully supported my local house of prostitution.

I believe that we all have a period of time that, in retrospect, is the best of all times. By that, I mean that everything is new and exciting. You have absolutely no worries; you only have yourself to hold accountable for whatever. You are having the time of your life; sometimes "the period of time" is only for a week or a month. For me, it had to be the year 1958.

That year, my good friend Evelio and I also joined the Nautical Club of Havana; we were on the "hunt" every Saturday afternoon, when the club held a dance called "Té Bailable"—loosely translated as Afternoon Tea Dance. This affair was appropriate for girls our age to be there in abundance and less supervised by their always vigilant parents or even chaperons.

I saw myself living "La Dolce Vita," normal for a nineteen to twenty year old, I thought. My friends and I (despite my mother's protest) continued to go out, amid a growing terrorist campaign of bombings and shootings between warring factions. Terrorist bombs going off in various establishments were as normal as the sound of the moving traffic, usually during the night and early morning, I guess to minimize the loss of human life. We did not pay much attention to any of this activity; we thought we were immortal and that nothing would ever happen to us.

I will never forget a Saturday night in 1958 when our friend Eduardo invited Oscar, Julio, and I to go to Cabaret Tropicana. I can picture "Gudelia"[3] coming down my street to pick me up; already in the car were Oscar, Julio, and of course, Eduardo. Eduardo was about five foot six, with light brown hair that wasn't too thick and a very white skin complexion. I do not think that he had to shave every day, and he wore glasses and was slender, but not skinny like me. Eduardo was older than us by about three to four years. Soft-spoken, he always spoke with the "knowledge" attributed to an older person, and he had a dry sense of humor, but a humor nonetheless. He had already graduated from Villanova University and was working as an accountant; he was also the proud owner of Gudelia.

Julio looked more mature than Oscar and I. He stood about five seven, and I think he was already shaving. He had dark brown hair that was a heavier texture than Oscar's thinner hair and sort of wavy. He always kept it short; he did not use the "greasy kid stuff" very popular in the 1950s. His skin complexion was light tan. He was not fat but a little husky. His voice sounded more mature with a certain ring of authority. He dated Oscar's sister for a while. Julio and I were also classmates at Saint Augustine College.

Oscar was about five six, with very smooth, medium tan skin. His hair dark brown hair had a light texture and was very straight—it looked oriental; without the help of the grease, it would stand up and fly in all directions. Oscar was a little chubby. I think it was hereditary. Oscar was very soft spoken; when he talked on the phone with his girlfriend, I could not hear a word. Oscar and I shared the same last name and were also classmates at Saint Augustine College.

I never forget the entrance at Tropicana—colored lights, a large fountain with the iconic dancer in the middle, the entrance under a lighted canopy where valets would take your car. I felt like I was a millionaire. It was kind of funny that little Gudelia was rubbing elbows with so many brand-new Cadillacs and Mercedes. It was amazing to me. Cabaret Tropicana was founded in the same year I was born, 1939; it did not look that old. Eduardo wanted to break in his brand-new Diners Club card at the famous night club. Cabaret Tropicana had two large sections—one under the crystal arches and the other under the stars.

That night, the dancer's show of the Cabaret Tropicana was in the open, under the stars! The dancers were just beautiful and very talented; they danced to typical Afro-Cuban rhythms, on specially built scaffolds that surrounded the dining area, and everyone was able to see the show no matter where you sat.

To make our night even more especial, we were going to see Nat King Cole[4] performing live! Wow! Nat was wearing a gold lamé jacket, gray pants, and two-tone shoes. What a show he gave us; his velvet voice sang all of our favorite songs—"Mona Lisa," "Dance Ballerina," "A Blossom Fell," "The Autumn Leaves." He even sang in Spanish! It was a night to remember. We had a great dinner—I forget what I had. We drank and saw many pretty women. I can close my eyes and relive the whole thing all over again. Tourists would pay hundreds of dollars just to be there.

Evelio and I had spent many good times together, even though Oscar, my school buddy, lived about a block away from me. Oscar expended a great deal of time visiting his girlfriend at her home. Lasi expended a considerable amount of time with migraines or brooding in his room about an issue with his previous girlfriend, so I wouldn't go out together with either Oscar or Lasi often.

Neither Evelio nor I remember exactly where—we think it was during a movie matinee at Los Angeles, a movie house in our neighborhood—we met Maggie and Nena.

Maggie was reddish blonde with an attractive face. She was built like a German trooper, not fat but heavy boned. Nena—that was her nickname; we never knew her real name—had a slender build, dark hair, a slightly dark complexion, and a very nicely proportioned body.

I do not recall Nena's mom, but I do remember Maggie's mother very well. Maggie's mom was about five foot six with a nicely shaped body. She had an attractive face and wore rimless glasses that were kind of round. I never saw her wearing any makeup, and she was always dressed very casually. She reminded me, well, she reminded me of a "Beatnik." At that time, Jean Paul Sartre's philosophy of existentialism was in full swing around the world; she was the hippie of her time. This was the first time I'd met someone who met the physical description, as portrayed in the movies, of a Beatnik; of course, we never mentioned our concept with her or her daughter.

Maggie and Nena did not live too far away from us—maybe about four blocks. We went to visit them often, and our evenings were full of pleasant conversation about typical teenage subjects. One evening, Evelio and I were on our way to visit Maggie and Nena.

"Evelio, let me ask you something." I stopped walking and looked at him.

"Yeah," he responded.

"How long have we been visiting Maggie and Nena?"

"Well, you know, I think about ... two months. Why?" he responded.

"Don't you think that is about time that we make the move with those two? After all, as you said, we have been going there for almost two months now. Don't you think that maybe we should try to get more out of this relationship?"

"Hmmm, I haven't thought about that yet." He paused. "But how are we going to ... I mean, how do we know which one of those two we are going for?" he asked me with an inquisitive look on his face.

"Okay, here, we are going to flip a coin. Let's go under the light of that lamppost."

"Oh, man, I think this is too much," he commented.

"I've got a quarter here. We'll flip it—heads, Nena, tails, Maggie, Okay? What's your take?" I said.

"I'll take ... heads," Evelio responded.

"Fine, mine is tails; there we go." I flipped the coin; the coin went up, shining on its way down in the light of the lamppost, and landed on my hand. As soon as the coin touched my hand, I placed the other hand on top; this would make for a more dramatic sense of expectation.

"Ready, Evelio, here we go." I took my hand off the coin.

"You drew Nena. I'll take Maggie. Let's go." We continued our walk to their apartment building; Maggie and Nena were neighbors in the same building, which was very convenient.

Evelio was still a little puzzled at such a weird arrangement, and then he asked me, "How do you know that Nena is going to go for me and Maggie, for you?"

"I don't know. We have to start somewhere. We'll go really slow, just watch how it goes. Then, if it seems that the coin made the wrong call, then we'll just switch girls. I think we are going to know pretty quickly. Don't worry about it." I do not think that Evelio was totally convinced about my strategy, but he went along anyways.

That night at Nena's and Maggie's, we started our conquests. By the time we left, Evelio was officially Nena's boyfriend, and Maggie was my girlfriend; the coin was right after all.

Of course, this did not drastically change anything; we were always under the watchful eye of the ever-present "chaperon," so the only thing that changed was that we could steal a kiss every now and then, and we were allowed to hold hands.

Chapter 3

Who Took My Prostitutes Away?

In my native country, the culture allowed for young men, sixteen and older—sometimes even at fifteen depending on the degree of puberty—to pay a visit to a house of ill repute. We had several of these "red zones" to choose from in the Greater Havana area. Some were better than others; the better ones were frequently visited by the Department of Health inspectors, a great relief for us users. They were a bit more expensive than the others, but what the heck, safety was always first.

There was a house near the Antonio Maceo monument,[1] right near a Mercedes Benz dealership, called La Casa de Maria (Maria's House). La Casa de Maria was a high-priced establishment; the cost was about fifty dollars per encounter—five times what we paid at our, so to speak, "watering holes." La Casa de Maria was located on a second floor building and even had a glass-enclosed where a potential customer could see the "soup d'jour." Why was the price so high? I was told that the girls were "crème de la crème." I never went there; actually, I never knew about this place. But some of my friends told me about it years later.

Between 1958 and early 1960, my friends and I frequented two or three of the same houses. The girls got to know us well. They knew us on first name basis, and they were nice and clean. Although there were no freebies, we always had a good time; the service was great!

We went very often, mostly on the weekend. What I

experienced one Saturday night, I do not think ever happened to any of my friends. As usual, Eduardo came to pick us up in Gudelia; you could only fit four people in this little car, so besides Eduardo, Julio, Oscar, and I piled in. Sometimes our conversations were single-minded.

"Hi, how is everybody?" Eduardo asked, turning his head toward us.

"I'm fine."

"I'm good."

"Great!" We all responded about the same time.

He was holding the car keys in his hand and said, "Before we get going, let me ask you something, okay?"

"Shoot!"

"I'm all ears."

"I'm listening."

"What do you guys think if we try somewhere new tonight?" Eduardo started.

"What do you have in mind?" Julio responded to the question with a question.

"Why do we have to change now?" Oscar asked, as if he was afraid that we were going to change our routine.

"Did you have a fight with someone since our last Saturday night visit?" I did my part, since everyone seemed to be answering questions with questions.

Nobody seemed to have an actual answer to any of these intriguing questions.

"What! Are you falling in love with someone in the house, Oscar?" I asked, turning my head to Oscar sitting next to me.

"Yeah, are you?" Eduardo directed his question at Oscar. It was picking on Oscar time.

"That is all we need now." Julio turned around in his seat, facing Oscar and finally breaking up the question session.

"No, guys, that's not what I mean," Oscar tried to respond, in an attempt to clear any misunderstandings, only to be interrupted by Eduardo.

"Okay, look, it's just that … I thought that, well … maybe we should try somewhere new, open our horizons, create new friends, that's all … experience new experiences." Eduardo looked around, hoping to get a consensus from all of us.

"It sounds good to me," I exclaimed in agreement.

"I'm all for it," Julio agreed as well.

"Are we still going to La Plaza del Vapor (the Vapor Plaza) for fried rice afterward?" said Oscar, sounding kind of worried that we may also change that part of our routine—a tall pile of freshly cooked, delicious fried rice for seventy-five cents and five cents for a Coca-Cola, a super bargain.

"Okay, guys, here we go," Eduardo said, starting Gudelia.

The "red light" district of the city that we all went to was fairly large. Our favorite street name was Pajarito (Little Bird), which was also the, loosely, "main street" of the district and, to the best of my recollection, a good two or three blocks long (which also makes me wonder who lived at either end of the district that was not part of the "profession"; just a thought). There were houses on both sides of the street. All the girls were inside. Nobody was outside hawking for customers; that was not allowed. And considering the business, it was relatively quiet all around.

The houses my friends and I patronized were nice and clean; the women were also pretty and clean. Prostitution in Cuba was not really legal, but the government and the authorities looked the other way, to the point that the Health Ministry would make sure no diseases were prevalent in these houses and that, at the very least, basic health precautions were being taken. Not all the houses received the same attention. There were others, less expensive, off the beaten path, and probably not known to the health ministry, as well as streetwalkers. I never touched that! I never met anyone who got sick from any of the brothels that my friends and I frequented in Havana.

We always visited the "houses" early; by that, I mean about 8:00 to 8:30 p.m. This way, we would find the girls fresh and ready to go. Eduardo had parked Gudelia nearby, so we walked to the district as usual. We went by our favorite houses, and fortunately, no one from inside saw us walking by.

After a serious debate, we decided to try a new house; it was nice inside, just like the ones we had visited on prior occasions. The place was clean; music playing, though not too loud; and the chairs and couches were comfortable, giving that "at home" feeling—of course you would not do this at home. We were approached by the matron, the person in charge of the girls; she received the monies and took care of any issues about the management of the place as well as the girls. The price was the same as at our usual spots—about ten or fifteen dollars; at that time, the Cuban peso and the dollar had the same street value, so they both circulated freely.

There were several "unoccupied ladies" now just sitting around. Our eyes always made the choices. They were all very nice-looking. I chose one among them. She introduced herself as Carmen, not that the name matters. Carmen was not her real name anyways, but hearing a name and being introduced made it more personal.

Carmen appeared to be in her early thirties. Her light brown, wavy hair slightly touched her shoulders, her skin was light, her eyes were hazel green, and her lips were full but not too thick. Her shapely, well-proportioned body was on a five foot five-frame. Although her legs were not long, they were neither slender nor heavy, so they seemed to fit her frame very well. Her face, what is a pretty face anyways? Of course one always looks at the face to see if it corresponds with one's interpretation of a pretty face. Invariably, we all have a standard that we use to give us an idea of what we consider to be a pretty face—for example, Audrey Hepburn, Elizabeth Taylor, Marilyn Monroe, and so on. Each one of these artist's faces had something pretty about them, but they were all different. There was something pretty about Carmen's face.

I always had the ability to remember faces, not names, faces. There was something familiar about Carmen, but how could that be? This was my first time here! She bid me to follow her into her bedroom, where we made love. Before we got cleaned up and got dressed, I always tried to engage in a little conversation, since I definitely did not want to be the first one sitting out there in the living room, waiting for my friends to come out.

"Why do you look at me like that?" Carmen asked inquisitively.

"I am sorry. I can't help it," I responded.

"Why?" she asked me, puzzled.

"Well I hope I don't upset you, but … I have this problem—"

"What! Are you gay?" she interrupted me.

"Oh no … no … my God, it's not that. It is just that I always remember a face … and think I know you; actually I'm sure I know you," I said cautiously.

"Really?" She was now intrigued.

"The worst part about it is that I know from where," I continued with my explanation.

"I'm listening." She sat on the bed next to me with her hands on her waist, her head cocked, her bare breasts pointing at me as if they were going to shoot me if I said something wrong.

"Well ...ahem," I said, clearing my throat. "Okay, I live in La Vibora; across from my apartment building there is a grocery store named Aragon. I'm sure that I have seen you there several times before," I finally responded.

"Hmmm," she responded with a smile in her eyes.

I knew that I was not really in trouble at this point. "Look, you don't have to worry about anything. My lips are sealed, and I'm not going to say anything to anybody about you. I understand that your way of life has nothing to do with your privacy. I respect that. I'm just that way." My words came out in a hurry to assure her that she did not need to worry.

"Thank you, I appreciate that," she said, lowering her arms from her waist. "Now, get out of my bed! I have work to do!" she said, snapping her fingers at me.

"I knew it; you got mad at me!" I said sitting up on the bed rather quickly.

"No, I already spent too much time with you ... unless, you want to pay for another round; I'm going to get in trouble," she said, smiling at me.

"Okay, okay! I'm moving!" I finished dressing.

To this day, I never told my friends anything about what happened. A few days after this incident, I met Carmen again at the grocery store across my apartment building. She was there with her young son. Our eyes met, and we just said hi to each other. I never took any advantage of knowing her way of life.

About mid-1960, "my Prostitutes" were taken away forever. I never saw Carmen or any of the others again. I am assuming that the "workers" were given "real" jobs somewhere in the "new society."

The Castro government closed all the houses because they represented, according to the Communist code of morals, the evils and exploitations attributed to capitalism. This was it! This really ticked me off. Nothing that had happened until this moment meant that much to me; now I was really concerned as to where my country was going! It was not immoral for the new order to take away someone's hard-earned property or put someone away for twenty years for disagreeing with the system or even place a person in front of a firing squad if he or she were considered "dangerous" to the cause.

The hypocrisy and irony of the "system" became evident under Castro's regime several years later, when young girls, due to economic conditions, became *jineteras*.[2] The jineteras walked the street in the known tourist areas and sold their bodies for money and, in some cases depending on immediate needs, according to friends of mine who have visited Cuba recently, for just articles of clothing.

In a Communist paradise, supposedly, there is no such thing as poor-, middle-, and rich-class distinctions but only the "new class."[3] The jineteras were a product of the system; they sold their bodies in order to improve the family circumstances, a tough decision to make for any parent. So much for a system that prides itself in always fighting for "human dignity and rights."—what hypocrisy

The promise of the worker's paradise was not working in Cuba.

Unfortunately for the Cuban people, the money earned by the tourist trade was not necessarily being used to improve citizen's lives. Just take a stroll through old Havana (if the Cuban authorities allow you), and you will see buildings falling apart, the infrastructure rotting away due to lack of maintenance. I wonder where the money is going—fomenting Latin American revolutions anyone?

The Castro government just looked the other way when young girls, and even young boys, "walked the streets" again. This time, the need for them was more basic—put food on the table. The "Socialist/Communist" hypocritical ideology of morality had taken my Prostitutes away, but it had also taken away people's dignity, for just a piece of bread and a pair of new panties.

Chapter 4

Deceit, Breakup, and a
New Year's Nightmare

Throughout 1958, my parent's relationship took a turn for the worse. The whole year had been full of arguments and uncomfortable situations; the most affected were my two sisters. I was somewhat in the margin due to my work and my outings with my friends; in retrospect, as the male of the house, I had the option of shutting down the whole situation from my mind by not being there. I had the feeling that my parents' separation or even divorce was a matter of time.

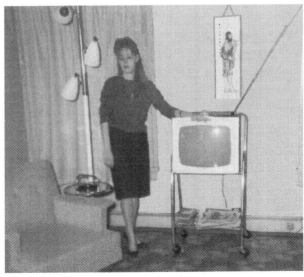

My older sister Ines.

My older sister, Inez, was instrumental in uncovering that my father was seeing another woman. We do not know for sure when the affair started, but we think it was soon after my father got his new job at Lamas Commercial Laundering Service.

We started getting our laundry done at Lamas, free of charge. Somewhere along the way, some of the clothing was coming back stained, but we did not know where the stains were coming from. My mother complained to my father about the situation, and he said that he would look into it. For a while, we did not receive any stained clothing, but they would start again and then mysteriously stop.

Then we started finding strange articles left at our door, and unusual stains appeared at out front door. Inez believed these were voodoo articles. We found about four of them. Of course, we got rid of them; our next-door neighbor, Mirtha, helped my sister clean up the door. Mirtha resided with her parents. She was about five foot six and had dark brown, curly hair. Her hips were kind of wide, and she had a big chest. I think she may have been in her early thirties.

During the last object drop, Mirtha saw a boy of about nine years old placing the object at our door. She scared him away, and that was the last time that we got any voodoo objects.

The next incident occurred when Inez and our aunt—Inez spent most of her time with my mother's younger sister, Caridad, at her variety store, La Flor del Casino (the Casino's Flower), located at the Casino Deportivo—decided to go shopping in downtown Havana. When the taxicab dropped them at a very popular shopping intersection, Inez saw my father's car driving by with a woman at his side; my sister did not say anything to my aunt Caridad at that time, or to my mother.

Several days went by. My father seemed to be working a lot, and we did not see each other that much. This issue was not a big deal for me since, during my growing years, my dad was not the type of dad to give me a baseball glove and play ball at the park. On the weekends, he was often doing some side job with clients that he had kept from his TV, radio, and appliances business, or so he claimed.

One Sunday, after my father had left to work with a client's TV, Zonia insisted that she wanted to be taken to downtown Havana to go to El Cinecito (the Little Movie House), a movie theater for children that featured cartoons and Walt Disney movies. So my mother took her there. After the movies, Zonia wanted to go to one of the parks by El

Malecon; we had not gone to the parks very often since we'd moved out of the city.

My mother and Zonia were walking toward the park when my mother received quite a shock. On the opposite side of the street, she saw my father facing her. He was holding a small child in one arm, and his other hand was holding another child. Adelfa, the woman he was seeing was standing next to him. Zonia was only six tears old at the time; when she saw her father, she let go of my mother's hand and ran after my father screaming, "Daddy, Daddy." Fortunately, there were no cars going by at that moment; it was a very dangerous situation. My mother was so shocked that she was not able to articulate anything.

But as soon as she got home, she started packing all my father's belongings. Zonia was very upset when she saw my mother packing my father's things. She really did not understand what was going on, but she called Inez and told her to come home, saying that Mother was packing her dad's things.

Inez came home from our aunt's shop and my mother related to her what had transpired that afternoon on the way to the park.

My father did come later that evening, but my mother did not allow him to come in. She handed him his bags and told him, "I don't want to see you, ever again!"

Inez was bent on finding out what kind of person would decide to break up a family. She borrowed $250 from our Aunt Caridad to pay for a private investigator to go after Adelfa and find out more about her. It took the investigator about a month to come out with photos and a report on Adelfa's activities. These photos showed her in the company of a metro bus driver, embracing and kissing him around the streets of downtown Havana. My sister took all these photos and went directly to my father's workplace, with the pretext that she wanted to talk to her dad. Instead, she went directly to Adelfa's workstation, and in front of her coworkers, she threw all the pictures and the reports in front of her shouting, "You are a whore!"

We never knew what happened after that incident at my father's workplace. Everyone around Adelfa saw the pictures as they lay on the floor; my father was attending a technical issue at that time, but the commotion that his daughter had caused was called to his attention. By the time he made it to Adelfa's workstation, Inez had left. We do not know what kind of explanation Adelfa gave him, but whatever she said apparently worked because my father eventually married her and had a son with her—a half brother that I never acknowledged. It took over twenty years for Inez and me to speak to our father again.

I guess that my father had made up his mind, but he waited, as not to spoil the Christmas holidays for us. He chose New Year's Eve, December 31, 1958, as the day for him to turn over a new leaf in life. I think I was home at the time. He came home from work, and he asked my mother to go to their bedroom since he needed to talk to her in private. They closed the door behind them. We could hear them talking, and then, after a while, we heard my mother crying. We found out later that my father had asked her for a divorce. This day turned out to be full of extraordinary events that affected my family deeply.

Incessant rumors had it that things were not going too well for the Batista regime, even though Batista's secret police and military intelligence agencies were doing a good job, through jailing, torturing, and eliminating those who were found to be linked or suspected of being connected with the rebel movements.

Fidel's rebels were getting closer to the city. As always, my mother continued to worry about me going out during so uncertain a political climate, with the exploding bombs and assassinations. She was always asking me not go out, so I stayed home New Year's Eve. My mother, even though she was not in any mood to celebrate anything due to her experience earlier in the day and my father leaving for good, joined my sisters and me and waited until 12:00 a.m. to eat the traditional "twelve grapes" and to drink a glass of cool cider, usually imported from Spain.

With the exception of Zonia, who was only six years old at the time, we were not ready to go to sleep yet. My mother and Inez stayed up with me to watch TV. Our TV volume was low at that time of the night. All of a sudden, we were distracted by an unusual noise outside. We could not immediately discern whether it came from outside our door or from down the street.

"Did you hear that? What is all that commotion out there? It's past one o'clock in the morning!" I remarked.

"I don't know. I think it's from Rodi's family across from us," Inez said.

"Don't go out; it could be dangerous." My mother, as usual, mother was being cautious and protective.

Rodi, his brother Emilio, and his parents—their dad was a personal chauffeur for an admiral in the Cuban Navy—lived in the apartment across the hall from us. Rodi spent at least 90 percent of his time visiting his girlfriend, Mirtha, so only went out with our group occasionally.

We opened the door leading outside our apartment to the hallway. The building complex was composed of two three-story structures with six apartments each, facing each other side by side, separated by an open balcony-hallway leading to the building stairs by a distance of about three to four feet. The front apartments had their own large balcony overlooking the street. Rodi's family's apartment was exactly across the way from ours. The door to their apartment was half opened; the family was all gathered in the living room, talking and acting very excited.

"Hey, Rodi, is everything okay?" I asked. "What's going on?"

"My dad just came home to tell us that Batista has fled the country! He said that it is very dangerous out there; the national police and the military intelligence organizations are in disarray. He is saying that we should stay indoors!" Rodi responded, very excited.

"Don't go anywhere!" Rodi's father said to us, standing at his door.

"But, I did not see any news about it on the TV," I said.

"They may not say anything until tomorrow so as to avoid panic," Rodi said.

"Oh, my God! I think that we should turn off all the lights and stay quiet for now; you never know what this event is going turn out to be," my mother said warily.

The TV station never broke its programming to tell us the news that Batista had fled the country soon after midnight. We definitely could not go to sleep after this news. I do not think that anyone had thought his government would break up so abruptly.

Within a couple of hours, we saw police cars and others from Batista's organizations, as our neighbors had warned us, going by our street and getting out of their patrol cars, guns in hand, looking around and talking. The cars were military, the men were in civilian garb, and they were well armed and looking for something. They seemed to be very disorganized. We all concluded that the situation was extremely dangerous, so we stayed out of sight. Eventually, we all went to sleep, hoping that whatever happened out there was going to improve conditions in our country. That night and the following night, we could hear gunshots fired in the distance.

My grandparents and aunts were living in Jatibonico, Camaguey

Province, at that time and in the path of Castro's rebels; I began to worry about them. My Aunt Salva, one of my father's sisters, told me a few days later that something amusing had happened in their hometown. There was a shootout the morning of January 1 around the sugar mill management housing where they all lived. My grandfather, named Desiderio, just like my father and I, was the chief engineer and in charge of the electrical engineering of the Jatibonico Sugar Mill; housing was provided to all the top managers of the mill. This shootout involved a group of Fidel's rebels shooting at nothing; there was no one opposing them. The shootout was so intense, my aunt told me, that they had to hide down in the basement.

During the following few days, the rebels started arriving, but Fidel and his group were still making their way from Oriente Province toward Havana, while the media was ratcheting up its propaganda to make these people look like gods.

The closest contingency was located at the Escambray Mountains in the Las Villas Province, two provinces west of Havana. These forces were under the command of Faure Chomon.[1] Trucks started to drive by our street en route to designated military posts. Castro's forces were still in the Oriente Province, but they were slowly heading toward Havana. "I think he wanted to make a triumphant and historic grand entrance, officially taking possession of the capital."

The media was having orgasms about the rebels and about Fidel making his way to Havana. The rebels were smelly, long-haired, bearded, and dirty. They drove by the hundreds by our street in military as well as private trucks and cars. We all cheered at them as they went by because, at that time, we saw them as our liberators. The first few days after Batista left, there existed a dangerous void in government, which could have easily led to chaos; but fortunately, there were very few incidents of violence and lawlessness.

About a week or so after January 1, 1959, and during the arriving activities into the capital by the rebels, a knock came at our door. My mother answered. Standing by the door was a bearded, long-haired, slender man in faded green fatigues. Hanging from his right side was a long barrel nickel revolver, much like the six shooters you would see in a western movie. The gun was too big for this man. At first, my mother did not recognize the man, but he was none other that than one of her own brothers, Francisco, aka Kiko.

Chapter 5

Women and Children Only

I always wondered what had actually happened during the first few hours of that same New Year's Eve night—while my mother and sisters and I were witnessing what was going on outside our door—to the families, friends, and close associates of Batista. Many of his close associates had not been able to escape el Che's firing squads, but other, equally important individuals who were wanted by Castro's men had been able to escape during the first hours of January 1, 1959.

It just seemed so sudden. What kind of information had Batista received that had made him believe that night was the night that he and his associates must run for their lives? I did not think that everyone around Batista was a criminal or had done something he or she should not be proud of.

Some of my questions were not answered about that fateful night until about 1991, when I met a lady who was to become my second wife, Martha, the daughter of a national police lieutenant colonel and close friend to Batista for many years.

Martha (Marty) was seventeen years old at the time, and she lived in El Vedado, a fashionable, middle-class section of Havana, with her parents and grandparents in a big, beautiful, Spanish style house. The following is an account she related to me of what had to have been a harrowing experience for a seventeen-year-old, on that very same night of January 1, 1959:

My grandmother was in the habit of throwing a big New Year's Eve party every year, where the entire family plus many,

many of our friends were invited. However, this year, it was different. The mood was not festive at all. In fact, it was somewhat sad. The situation in Havana was getting worse and worse as days went by. There was a lot of discontent, especially among the younger crowd. My parents made sure not to talk about these things in front of me, as to not upset me, but I knew things were very bad within Batista's government. There was a lot of tension, a lot of concern among every one associated with the Batista government.

That 1958 New Year's Eve, our family and I gathered around the dining room table and had an ordinary dinner. There was no party this year! We watched some TV and went to bed. My father had been called earlier for duty.

Much later that same evening, my mother came into my room. "Wake up, honey, wake up and get dressed quickly!' My mother shook me to wake me up. 'We have to go!' She looked very frightened.

Startled, I jumped off my bed. "Go ... where, Mom?" I asked, still a little dazed.

"Batista just left the country, and your father called to tell me we had to join him at the Columbia Military Airport right away!" my mother told me hurriedly, almost in tears. "Just gather some clothes and anything of value that you wish to take with you—not too much. Hurry up!"

"But ..." I thought of my dog. "What about Blanquita?" I asked, still a little confused.

"She'll have to stay with your grandparents," she responded. "Come on. The driver your father sent to pick us up is waiting outside to take us to the military airport."

My father, Oscar, had sent one of his most trusted drivers from his police station, a man nicknamed Gallo Prieto (Black Rooster), and put him in charge of picking us up. Gallo Prieto was a very skillful driver, and he was also a very impetuous man; my father trusted that he would get us to the airport safely, and that he, if necessary, would defend us with his life.

Gallo Prieto sped through the empty streets of Havana to get us to the Columbia Military Airport as quickly as possible. All the way to the military airport, I could not help but noticed how quiet the streets of Havana were, considering that it was New Year's Eve. I was so scared that my teeth were hitting against each other. I kept thinking, *Why am I running away like a criminal? I haven't done anything wrong!*

My father had already left in Batista's airplane by the time we made it to the military airport. Gallo Prieto escorted my mother and me to the tarmac, where a paratrooper military airplane was at ready with engines roaring. There was a little bit of waiting for one of the men who was in the field to attach a ladder for the women and the children to board the plane.

A high-ranking military person was left behind to protect us. He was to make sure that all the wives and children would indeed be able to get into this airplane.

At that instant, two men standing around waiting to be able to board the airplane and leave the country proceeded to desperately climb up into the airplane, ahead of the women and children still boarding. The officer took out his weapon, fired a couple of shots into the air, and said very loudly, "This airplane is only for the wives and the children of the men that have left already. I will personally shoot any of the men who try to get into this plane!"

Since the plane was a paratrooper's airplane, there were no seats except the side metal benches along which the paratrooper's would normally sit until it was time to jump. We all sat on those cold, hard metal seats all the way to Santo Domingo. Little children were crying, and their mothers tried to soothe them unsuccessfully. Some of the women were sobbing, while others would talk to each other. I was sitting next to a little boy who was about three years old and played with him to keep him from crying, while his mother took care of his two little sisters. It was a very exhausting trip, and on top of everything, there was no bathroom!

When we arrived in Santo Domingo, I told my mother that I had to go to the bathroom very badly; my bladder was so full that it hurt. I located the ladies' room at the airport, and it took me a long time to be able to relieve myself.

President Alfonso Trujillo, who was the dictator of the Dominican Republic at that time, gave asylum to Batista's party, until such time that they would decide where they were going to settle permanently. My father met us at the airport, and my mother and I began to cry. It was an emotional scene.

Finally after this ordeal, we were taken to a very nice hotel in the city, where Batista himself was staying. Trujillo paid all our expenses; we were all accommodated in very nice rooms with two double beds. That was the beginning of my new life away from Cuba, my country of birth.

We stayed in Santo Domingo for about a month. Sometime toward the end of our stay there, my father began to insist that it was safe for my mother and me to go back to Cuba in order to try to regain our property, to no avail, and for me to finish high school; his insistence was a little strange to me. Later, I found out the truth as to why my father was so insistent on us leaving Santo Domingo so quickly. Somehow, he had gotten wind about Trujillo's son's plan; apparently, he had taken a liking to me and was making plans to lure me and take me to his farm!

My mother and I left for Cuba, while my father went to Mexico to start all the paperwork to move us permanently to the United States, our final destination. My uncle by marriage to my mother's sister, who happened to be in the Castro government, and some other friends were waiting for us at Havana's Marti International Airport. My uncle took us quickly back to his house.

My mother stayed in Cuba only long enough to arrange things left undone, gather some important documents, and then left Cuba again to join my father in Mexico.

I moved to my grandparents and aunt's apartment in El Vedado. By then, the Castro government had confiscated my grandfather's beautiful Spanish house. I went back to school in Cuba. I had one more year to finish high school. While I was in Cuba, I tried to live a somewhat normal life—mind you, not the life I was accustomed to; that was gone forever! Nevertheless, I went out with my friends and a new boyfriend.

By the time I graduated from high school, my parents had been able to leave Mexico and had headed for the United States with their Permanent Resident Cards in hand. A soon as they arrived in the States, they claimed me as their daughter. In a matter of just weeks, I joined them in Miami. And that is how our new life began in this wonderful country, "America, the beautiful."

Chapter 6

A New Sheriff in Town

The forces fighting in the Escambray were commandeered by Dr. Rolando Cubelas and Faure Chomon. By the end of 1958, several thousand rebels had gathered in the mountains. My uncle Francisco had a rank of sergeant and spent nine months in the Escambray as a medic. His commander sent him twice to Havana for secret missions. His code name was Raul, and he came to visit us during one of those missions.

People looked at us a little differently. Not everyone had a family member in the rebel forces. Especially surprised were my friends who lived in the apartment across from ours, the ones whose father had been a personal driver for a Cuban Navy admiral under Batista; another uncle of theirs was a member of the secret police. They never gave my family or me any reason to distrust them; nevertheless, we had always been careful not to discuss anything political with them during the Batista years. We were proud of having a "Barbudo" (bearded one), as we called the rebels, staying with us.

It is worthy to note the general view, from my perspective, that in the beginning, people my age saw this change in government as something that in an idealistic way would help us get rid of oppression and improve our lives. People felt free, and everything looked and felt different; everybody looked up to these bearded heroes who risked their lives in the mountains to save us from the tyranny of a dictatorship.

People were mesmerized by the lengthy Castro speeches; women were orgasmic at the sight of him, and of any of these barbudos. Men started to wear their hair long, grew beards, and wore black berets, just like "el Che"; everybody wanted to get into the act. As far as I was concerned, I eventually took a skeptical view of this whole experienced after I started working with my uncle Francisco at the CTC (Confederation of Cuban Workers).

At the beginning of the revolution, it was typical of rebel officials to "intervene" or "take possession" of organizations, buildings, cars, and properties. These steps were designed to avoid chaos; taking control of organizations was an essential step for the setting stage for the new government. Francisco—at this point, just like all rebel forces, he was wearing the olive green fatigues—was given a job at the CTC, the umbrella organization that represented all the Cuban worker unions. The CTC building was located in the center of Havana City, and it was the national headquarters for all unions. Francisco was a barber by profession; his commanding officer assigned him to the Barbers and Beauty Salons Union on January 2, 1959, as national secretary organizer of the union.

Since my uncle's rebel organization, the Second Front Escambray, had been the first to march into Havana, it was only logical that he was provisionally placed in charge of the Barbers and Beauty Salons Union at the Cuban Workers Conference. About two weeks after being placed with this union, my uncle called on me to help him out with the collection of the union dues.

When Francisco recruited me to help him with this new position at the CTC complex, I had, by then, left Madedera Vigia and had taken a position with J. Gallareta & Company, a bottler and distributor of Rum Matusalem. Rum Matusalem was a manufacturer of quality rums since 1872, originating in Santiago de Cuba. The J. Gallareta & Company aged, bottled, and distributed in Havana the original Matusalem recipe brand, as well as other varieties of the rum. Rum Matusalem claimed that their recipe was then eighty-seven years old. Today, Rum Matusalem is being marketed throughout the United States, Latin America, and Europe. I am not sure, but just like Bacardi, Rum Matusalem left Cuba and settled in Mexico, where it competed with the Bacardi brand. In fact, the J. Gallareta was located not far from the Bacardi building. My job was in the data processing department.

After a few months at Matusalem, I had begun regretting leaving

Madedera Vigia. I was not too happy with this job because I felt that my chances to work myself up to a new position were very limited. The D P department was run by Teresa, a woman who had a great deal of experience with their Burroughs accounting machine system. Teresa was very well "positioned" with Mr. Jose Gallareta, the owner and manager of the company. Neither Teresa nor Mr. Gallareta seemed interested in training me on their Burroughs system. I could not compete with her body—Teresa had the face of a horse, but she was built like a "brick house"—so by the time my uncle contacted me, I had also left the J. Gallareta & Company and was in the process of looking for a new job.

At the CTC Barbers and Beauty Salons Union, I was given one of the best, if not the best, zones for collecting the union dues, El Vedado. El Vedado, a suburb of Havana, was middle- and upper-middle-class residential area and it hosted many well-known hotels, such as the Riviera, the Hotel National, and the Havana Hilton—renamed Havana Libre (Free Havana) by the Castro regime.

One of my favorite collections sites was a place called La Rampa (The Ramp). La Rampa was a little known concept in the '50s and the precursor of the "mall." La Rampa housed an entertainment and business center, a movie theater, CMQ, one of the largest Cuban radio and TV networks, several radio stations, night clubs, restaurants, and many barbershops and beauty salons, and other boutique shops.

I had the task, besides collecting dues, of creating goodwill and cooperation among the members at large; they were very suspicious of the union due to a history of corruption. We were going to change for the best, and the new government would make sure that corruption was a thing of the past—little did I know. While other collectors reported that they were encountering a rough time from the members, I always collected 80 percent of my zone.

I do not remember for sure when, but about three to four months later, a new dynamic began to unfold. One day, I had brought in the dues I'd collected for the day to the union building. Before I left for home, my uncle called me aside and told me not to go and collect the dues the following day and to stay home that evening. He had received a tip that elements of the Cuban Communist party wing of the Barbers and Beauty Salons Union's members were going to take over the union operations. Political takeovers were never carried out very peacefully.

My uncle spared me from a violent situation that following night;

there was a shooting at the CTC building. My uncle was given a position as a guard at the Commerce Ministry, where he worked for one and half years. He feared that, even rebels who had participated in the revolution but were not willing to blindly follow the leanings toward the left of the Castro government were destined to be blindsided by the revolution. Francisco realized that he was mistrusted by his peers and was not regarded as loyal to the "big picture."

My uncle was removed from his position at the Barbers and Beauty Salons Union and ended up with a job in the new revolutionary police department, guarding the Commerce Ministry building. As for me, I was glad for the experience, but a very uneasy feeling began to brew in my mind.

I never went back to the CTC building. In less than three days, the Cuban Communist Party took over the Barbers and Beauty Salons Union, as well as other unions. The official explanation from the authorities was, "In the new revolutionary Cuba, all parties have the right to participate in government."[1]

After the CTC and the Barbers and Beauty Salons Union debacle, I found myself again looking for a job.

The 26th of July Movement (Castro's rebel group) was the largest, and it was becoming the "de facto" political influence in the country; other rebel groups were either being assimilated or disbanded. From my perspective, I began to realize that Cuba was moving to a very uncomfortable place in history.

I was not open to the idea of trying to get a job in government, and I definitely did not want to be pressured into joining the militia or shouting "Viva Fidel" in the almost weekly "voluntary revolutionary rally"; "Cuba, Sí, Yankee, No!"

Finding work in the private sector was becoming ever more difficult; the private sector was disappearing at an alarming rate. I thought I would try the lumber company again, so I paid a visit to Matias; to my surprise, he told me that he could start me right away. I do not remember what day of the week it was when I went to see him; for all practical purposes I started on the following Monday. It was now early 1960. As it turned out, almost a year later, it was a good thing for me to get my job back at the Madedera Vigia, for my family's safety and my own.

During the last seven or eight months of 1959, I had managed to complete an intensive English course while English was still being taught in Cuba. I completed my course on September 21, 1959. I wanted to make sure that I would not forget the language; since I had graduated from Saint Augustine, I had no longer been involved with the English language. Also during these months of 1959, the nationalization process was moving along very rapidly.

Large foreign companies and companies that had ties to the United States, such as oil companies, electric and telephone companies, and agricultural companies were being nationalized[2] at a rapid pace. As its next step in the process of socializing Cuba, the Castro government made a move for the large and medium Cuban-owned companies—a move known as "Intervenir" (Confiscate).

The unions were on their way to being 100 percent under the control of the Cuban Communist Party. Unions eventually became irrelevant, as they are in most Communist countries. You could not mess with your employer, "the government"; if you did, you were labeled counterrevolutionary—hurray for freedom!

Just a few months after the arrival of the rebels, Fidel began to organize a worker's militia army, "defenders of the revolution." I was a little upset when I saw my father wearing the militia's uniform, but soon I understood that, when his company was confiscated (taken away from the rightful owners) by the government, he had no choice but to "show support" for the revolution and "voluntarily" join the militia.

I always wondered how so many militia uniforms were available for so many thousands of volunteers so quickly. Were all the clothing factories in Cuba working day and night putting together these uniforms? On the other hand, had this militia been conceived way beforehand?

The militia's uniform was full of symbolism—something created out of a typical Communist manual. The pants were olive green, symbolizing the people's readiness to defend the motherland; the blue worker's shirt symbolized that the Cuban blue-collar working-class was part of the revolution; the black beret, well I don't know what the black beret symbolized. El Che wore a black beret—hmmm? The militias received training in different kinds of weapons supplied by the Soviet Block, as well as basic defensive urban and field tactics.

The lumber company had changed for the better since I had left. The office had been expanded; a new floor had been built above the original office, next to the office of the company controller, Mr. Beltran. In addition, the company had two new employees—an office accountant,

Alfredo and a new office person, Ramon, who had been hired to do the collecting I had previously done. Ramon was about five foot eight. He had straight blond hair and was kind of a nervous guy—very easy to frustrate. I was given the task of being Alfredo's assistant.

Alfredo had just recently graduated from Havana University as an accountant and had been recommended to Matias by either a friend or family member. Alfredo was a short, balding man, with a sort of a pear-shaped body. He was very white, and I do not think that he ever went to the beach in his life. Alfredo was not old, maybe in his late twenties or early thirties. Because of his baldness, he let his hair grow long and combed it across the top of his head. He had a high-pitched voice that was very annoying. I could tell this guy had issues.

Alfredo showed up to work one morning, to everyone's surprise, in his brand-new militia uniform. We all looked at him with incredulity. So far, Alfredo was the only one in the lumber company who had joined the militia up to this point, and I expected others to follow.

Mr. Beltran, the company's controller, and I somehow connected. We became friends and got along very well. I am not sure exactly how old he was, but he was in his early sixties. He was about five foot seven, maybe a little taller; was slender, and had straight, thinning, gray hair that grew together with his original dark blond hair. He used to come to the office to check the company books about once a month. I remember the first time that he and I went out; he invited me to accompany him to get a bite to eat for lunch. Lunchtime in Cuba was about two hours, and many stores would close for lunch and reopen later.

"Do you like ham sandwiches?" he asked.

"Yeah, I do," I responded.

"You are not going to believe this ham sandwich," he said, as if he knew something really good and wanted to share it with me.

"Okay, what's in it?" I asked.

"Ham." He turned his head to me with a twinkle in his eye.

"No, I mean like what kind of ham?" I said.

"I'd rather wait till you try it," he responded.

We were lucky. We found a parking space not too far away from the sandwich shop. I don't remember the name of the shop, but it was somewhere in the center of downtown Havana. We sat down by the bar and were quickly attended by the waiter.

"Do you want to have a beer with your sandwich?" Mr. Beltran asked me.

"Sure, that sounds really good," I said.

The waiter came back with a couple of sandwiches, piled high with ham and Swiss cheese and cut at an angle, still warm after being placed in a "hot iron". If you have ever been to Miami or South Beach and had a Cuban sandwich (ham, roasted pork, Swiss cheese, a pickle and plenty of mustard), then you know what I'm talking about.

"So ... what do you think?" Mr. Beltran asked, looking at me inquisitively.

"This is a really good ham. What makes it so good?" I asked him.

"This ham is imported from Poland. The brand name is Kraukus. It's not cheap, but let me tell you, it's worth every bite," he said, sounding happy that he was able to share his find with someone who appreciated it as much as he did. This ham of his wasn't easy to find; I found the Kraukus brand when I lived in Connecticut and, later, when I moved to Miami. Kraukus is the ham I use for my special occasions.

"Absolutely delicious," I said after taking another bite with delight.

The conversation then turned to a more serious topic. It seemed he wanted to talk me in private, away from the lumber company environment. "So, tell me, Desi, what is your opinion about Alfredo joining the militia?" he asked after we'd enjoyed our ham sandwiches for a few minutes.

"May talk freely, Mr. Beltran?" I said, ready to give my honest opinion.

"Yes you can, but don't call me Mr. Beltran, just call me Carlos, okay?" He took another sip of his beer and smiled.

"Well, I think he is a real idiot, for lack of a better word, but I also think that there is something strange about that guy," I responded.

"What makes you think that?" Carlos asked.

"Okay, let me tell you this. A few weeks ago, all of us were having a little break in the afternoon. The guy who comes around selling Cuban coffee had just left. I don't recall how it came about, but during the conversation, Julio alluded to the fact that, when he was young, he had an accident and he suffered a cut on the head of his penis." I looked up at Carlos. "What do you think Alfredo said?"

"What did he say?"

"We are all going, gee-whiz, that's too bad. Can you get laid? Can you pee? Can you jerk off? Alfredo asked him, 'Can I see it?' I think that Julio was pulling everybody's legs."

Carlos just looked at me, tilted his head, and opened his eyes wide.

"That's not the only thing," I added. "I think he's doing something with the books."

"Do you really think so?" Carlos paused for a moment and then said, "I do too. I can't put my finger on it yet. Let me tell you something confidentially. Matias also suspects him," he said, lifting his hand as if to say, who knows?

"I also think that he joined the militia to protect himself. I don't like what is going on in this country. I had a chance to work with my uncle, a rebel with the Escambray group, in the CTC's Barbers and Beauty Salons Unions. One day, the Communists took over, just like that." I snapped my fingers. "I think that something really ugly is brewing in this country." I took another bite of my sandwich.

"How much do you know about a Communist takeover?" Carlos asked.

"Not much. I have never been very political until now; I only worried about having a good time," I responded.

"If I recommend a couple of books to read, would you read them?" Carlos asked me, his tone of voice low.

I looked at him somewhat inquisitively and then replied, "Yes, I would read them."

"Okay, these three books will give you a good perspective and insight into how leftists or a Communist ideology will manage to take over a country, or this country for that matter, very quickly."

"Wait; let me jot down the names of the books on this napkin," I said as took my pen out of my shirt pocket.

"*The New Class, Animal Farm,* and *The Church of Silence.* I hope you can find them; they are not going to be around much longer."

I wrote on my pad.

Carlos the auditor was the first person to tell me that we were on our way to become a Socialist-Communist country. I was able to find those three books. *Animal Farm* was written by George Orwell. *The New Class* was written, to my surprise, by a Yugoslav, Milovan Djilas. Djilas actually helped Tito[3] to unite the Balkan countries into one nation, Yugoslavia. After the fall of the Soviet Union, the Balkan countries then separated into the original independent countries that had existed before World War II—Croatia, Bosnia Herzegovina, Montenegro, Serbia, and others.

The Church of Silence, by Theodoric Zubek, was about the Catholic Church in Slovakia and the strategies with which it dealt with the procedures utilized by the Communists to seize control, not only over its property but over its doctrine, as the Communists silenced the teaching of the church and Czechoslovakia became part of the infamous "Iron Curtain." As I read, I began to be aware of how the Castro government had approached its takeover; what I learned from those books would never leave me. Sure enough, they were right on the money.

The controlled media gave to the public the general impression that the government was protecting the rights of the employee against the greedy and exploiting corporations, which were looking out for the US imperialism and its interests. The following example is one of the ways that it worked during the early days of the revolution:

Here is the gig—employees of the target corporation would complain to the press and the union that the company they worked for was taking advantage of them by paying low wages or in some other way. Next, people would march up and down in front of the targeted establishment—Lenin referred to this kind of mob and behavior by the populace as "useful idiots"—with a variety of signs proclaiming the "unfairness" of the situation. These signs would include banners that read things like, "Cuba, Sí. Yankee, No," and the like. Some of the marchers probably did not even work at the company they were protesting, but the demonstration looked good on TV.

After the protest had lasted a couple of days, the takeover was as good as done. The modus operandi of carrying this out was the same at all the targeted businesses. One morning, you would come to work, and several militiamen would be guarding the door, armed with .9mm Czechoslovakian-made submachine guns. Some of the militiamen may even be employees of the targeted company. The entrance door would be closed, paperwork started, and a couple of days later the company would be "confiscated by the workers," and the employees would become "owners" of the company.

The non-militia employees and the managers of the confiscated company, who had experience and knew how the company functioned, would not be allowed into the premises ever again. This was an insidious plan to place the business sector under government operation, a quick way to destroy the private sector. The displaced managers and employees would then buy a one-way ticket to Miami or New York. For all practical purposes, the government was now running the company—case *closed!*

In the next few months, it was somewhat stressful for me at the lumber company. Ninety percent of our customers were furniture makers and carpenters—business owners. Castro had created a new government entity, Instituto Nacional de la Reforma Agraria (INRA). INRA was a kind of industrial development agency that began to suck up all kinds of materials, such as wood, cement, and a number of others. Meanwhile, imports and materials were getting more and more difficult to obtain.

Our customers had a hard time finding materials for their businesses. Many of them recognized what was going on; some of them, out of frustration and feeling double-crossed by the revolution, were selling counterrevolutionary bonds to raise cash for groups already fighting against the Castro regime.[4]

It had been barely two years since Batista had left the country, and Fidel had taken over. I helped the customers sell counterrevolutionary bonds, right in front of Alfredo's nose, now a converted militia-accountant; of course, he did not know what the hell was going on. I also sold, as a cover, bonds for the Colombian guerrillas. These bonds financed the guerrillas being trained by Castro, with the purpose of bringing "true democracy" to Colombia— I think I am going to puke. I cannot recall the name of the guerilla group, but I think it may still be active in Colombia. Had I been caught selling anti-Castro bonds, I would have won a sure ticket to be shot by firing squad.

I did not support the new sheriff in town. I concluded that it was time to get the hell out of here!

Chapter 7

Looking for a Way Out

It was now the mid-1960s, and Evelio and I continued to see Maggie and Nena. We were of a mind-set that we were not going to let events around us interfere with our having fun. We watched the path the revolution had taken, saw that the government had taken our Prostitutes away; we did not know when we were going to be forced to stop having fun entirely.

By the time 1960 was coming to a close, the evidence that a political change in Cuba was occurring very quickly was mounting and very clear to me. The so-called Agrarian Reform[1] had taken property from legitimate landowners and distributed it to poorer farmers, eventually combining these properties into co-ops, following the Soviet pattern. The Urban Reform would take away an apartment building from the original and rightful owner; the residents would become the new "owners" of the apartment, and everybody would cheer! Private homes of exiled Cubans were being distributed among the new "elite."

Intense propaganda against the Catholic Church, especially with Catholic members was another part of Castro's takeover strategy. This made no sense at all, since 90 percent of the population was Catholic or professed to be Catholic. Somehow, Castro linked Catholics with the effort to get back to a Cuba before Castro. The propaganda strategy was so well executed that people started replacing the picture of Jesus in their homes with a pictures of Fidel or El Che—totally amazing! The brainwashing was so good that, when Castro declared, sometime in the 1960s, that Cuba was an atheist state, it seemed that nobody cared or made any waves about it.

Castro convinced the people that the Cuban Revolution must be defended from all foreign interest, especially from American imperialism. He built a large militia composed of working men and women; the total number of the militia reached two hundred and fifty thousand. This same militia force, about thirty thousand strong then, would repel our attack during the Bay of Pigs invasion. Persistent rumors insisted that a military invasion[2] was in the works. Meanwhile, the militia became a very handy tool to squash any immediate or future internal popular rebellion, as the Socialist-Communist process continued.

Havana began to be filled with trenches, Soviet- and Czechoslovakian-made anti-aircraft guns, Stalin tanks, and an array of Soviet-supplied military equipment. Fidel also insisted that the Americans, after confiscation and nationalization of all of their business interests in Cuba, were going to invade Cuba any day now. This claim was also used to tighten up the screws to all potential political dissidents. Fidel still claims today, from time to time, that Americans are going to invade Cuba.

There was some early talk of Castro holding national elections in the near future, but not before the revolution had been secured. It was all about taking control and imposing his brand of Communist-socialism.

The old established Cuban press was disappearing. One of the oldest and most prestigious conservative newspapers in this hemisphere, *El Diario de la Marina* (*The Marine Daily*), was in serious trouble with the Castro government, and it was eventually closed. *Avance* (*Advance*), another leading Cuban daily, was confiscated, as well as *El Mundo* (*The World*). The few remaining free presses were disappearing very rapidly.

The new so-called "free press," such as the daily, *Revolución* (*Revolution*), the official government newspaper, started a heavy campaign against *El Diario de la Marina* and *El Mundo*, accusing the papers of criticizing the revolution and serving American interests. The Castro government claimed that these foreign interests wanted to go back to the Batista dictatorship. Revolutionary newspapers, such as *Revolución*, *Granma*, and *Hoy*—a daily established in the early thirties, *Hoy* (*Today*), was the official Cuban Communist party newspaper—were replacing these old and well-established newspapers. The new "free press," not to mention TV and radio, only reported and voiced news and propaganda favorable to the revolution. So much for exercising the right of free speech.

For many years, Radio Kramer had played only American music, to the benefit of a large and growing American community living in Havana. During my teens, I listened to Radio Kramer every day, enjoying a good variety. During the day and into the evenings, the station played Glenn Miller, Artie Shaw, Benny Goodman, and others. My favorite radio show, *The Hit Parade*, was broadcasted on Saturday evenings about 7:30 p.m. It kept me current with the top 40s American songs and artists of the week. My all-time favorite artist was Bill Haley and the Comets; I dropped tons of nickels in the jukebox playing "Rock around the Clock." He was followed by Elvis, Sammy Davis Jr., Frank Sinatra, the Platters, Nat King Cole, and others. Now, Radio Kramer was gone!

Musicians were prohibited from playing the saxophone because it represented the "decadent capitalist bourgeois."

My favorite American magazines, *Life, Look, Movie Life, Hit Parade, Reader's Digest,* and many others that Havana's newsstands had once sold had just disappeared. Soviet propaganda magazines, which pretended to look like American magazines, were replacing them at the newsstands. You could still get *The New York Times,* which was always very accommodating with the Castro regime.

It was becoming more and more difficult to find supplies that we Cubans were used to—American cigarettes, food products, home products, office supplies. American cars became *frozen* in time! I believe that 1959 or 1960 was the last year that American cars were imported and sold in Cuba.

During the 1950s, the Cuban economy had been growing strong, despite the rebels, the uncertainty of terrorist acts, and the assassinations. In fact, Cuba, according to an extensive economic study conducted in 1952, economy wise was only second to the United States in the American continent. Cuba had a growing manufacturing industry and was a top exporter of sugar, tobacco, and coffee.

The country was home to many service companies and a healthy number of small business entrepreneurs. Unfortunately, these industries started to disappear also. Cuba had something else very rare in Latin American; it was the only country besides the United States with a defined middle-class citizenry.

The drain of experienced business owners, managers, and professionals continued unabated. Once their businesses had been confiscated or nationalized and placed in the control of the employees, these men and women began to leave Cuba in droves, heading for Miami, Puerto Rico, Mexico, Venezuela, Spain, and other countries. This was the beginning of "Little Havana" and the growth of the metropolis of Miami as it is known today.

At the lumber company, although we did not talk about it, tension was building up slowly; already a couple of the lot workers, pressured by their peers, had decided to join the militia. I was sure that it was just a matter of time before the government would intervene in the lumber company.

When I got home from work, I had to deal with the ever-present Comité de la Defensa de la Revolución (CDR)[3] person in my building, always watching what we did, who we talked to, and who came to visit us. I knew, as the revolutionary process advanced, that it was only a matter of time before I would be called to take sides.

Most every day after work and before dinner, I would sit on a division of our apartment building entrance, a two-foot high wall between the two attached buildings, which faced each other. The bus stop was just a few yards away. And if Lasi was not having one of his migraines, we would sit there and chat for a while; the time might have been between 5:30 p.m. and 6:30 p.m.

One day, I saw Lasi's brother, Emilio, aka Chichi. Chichi was Lasi's brother, about two years younger than him, not as tall as Lasi, dark complexion, but not as dark as Lasi was. Chichi was coming down the street with his new militia uniform on, I do not know what happened to me, but I went ballistic. "What the hell are you doing with that stupid uniform on?" I exclaimed in front of everyone waiting for the bus.

"I am ready to defend the revolution from the Americans invaders!" Chichi responded.

"So, you too believed that crap!" I responded.

"You better get yourself behind the revolution and stop defending the American imperialism," Chichi responded in an aggressive tone.

"And since when do you know so much about imperialism. What about Russia? They took over all the countries to their west. The people can't get out if they want to," I fired back, Chichi just looked at me dumbfounded.

"So in other words, Castro's government is going to suspend the guarantees of our Constitution, just like Batista did, in that case then what have we gained?" I continued.

Meanwhile, the people waiting for the bus were just looking at our argument, and no one, to my surprise, said anything.

"The Russian are our friends," Chichi responded.

"Well, let me tell you something, Fidel said that we are free to express our opinions and views. You said that, if I don't get behind the revolution, I am an imperialist. So where is my freedom to express my opinion? I see that they already washed that little brain of yours. I think that you are a real idiot. Good luck with your stupid militia," I responded. I walked away and took the stairs up toward my apartment, before the CDR showed up.

***

A year had gone by, and still, I was not joining the militia. I was not enthusiastic about the revolution at all. If given the opportunity, I would not refrain from making unfavorable comments to my friends and coworkers about the revolution. This really was not a good idea, for I had identified myself as a potential counterrevolutionary. Besides I already had a few "marks" against me. I was a member of the Catholic Church, active in catholic organizations, and a graduate of an American school—in other words, according to the "new order," someone to keep an eye on.

I suppose that I could have accepted the revolution premise and joined the militia as some of my friends from school did. After all, my background was in demand by the new elite. Eventually, as I had moved up the ranks, I would have been given a brand new Lada—a Soviet version of the Italian Fiat—or maybe even a Peugeot 404, plus a confiscated apartment in New Havana, or maybe even a confiscated home in my old stomping grounds of El Vedado. I would have received the best of health care, only available to the "elite." But at what price? I would have had to give up my convictions, my values and sell my soul to the devil.

My mother knew me well; she knew that my mouth would eventually get me in trouble. She talked with my father to see if my uncle Enrique, his brother, could find me a job with his employer. Uncle Enrique's employer was Garcia Line Inc. He had been working with Garcia for several years and had the position of chief engineer on one of their ships.[4] My mother and father were trying to get me out of Cuba before my mouth got me in trouble.

One evening after supper, I went downstairs as usual to meet with my friends and have a conversation—TV had not yet taken the place of interactions with human beings. No one was there. Lasi was still inside his apartment, and Rodi was probably already near his beloved Mirtha's house trying to spend a few minutes with her. So I just sat on the small divider wall, about a foot high, along a hallway that divided our buildings. I entertained myself by watching the people at the corner waiting for Route 14 to take them to their destination. I lit a cigarette; I still had a few packs of American cigarettes stashed away. Maybe about ten minutes had passed when I saw Evelio coming down the street to join me.

"Hi, Evelio. How are things going?"

"Okay. Where is everybody?" Evelio responded.

"I don't know. Lasi is still having supper. I think Rodi is you know where. It's just as well. I have wanted to talk to you privately anyway. Let's walk up Lacret Street. I want to tell you something very important."

Evelio looked at me very inquisitively, not knowing what to expect from me. He still remembered the deal about Maggie and Nena.

We crossed the street toward the grocery store and started walking on Lacret. About three blocks away was the street where Los Angeles Movie Theater was located.

"Do you want a cigarette?" I asked him, taking out of my pocket a box of Winston, my favorite American cigarette.

"Okay, so … what is all the mystery?" Evelio asked.

"Well, you know that Lasi and his brother, who is now a militiaman, at this point, are pro-revolutionaries. And Rodi, well … Rodi is too involved with Mirtha. I don't think he would be interested in what I want share with you. Besides, I'm very comfortable to tell you what I'm about to tell you, because honestly, you are the only one I can trust." I was beginning to distrust my other friends as well as my neighbors.

"Okay, I'm listening," he said, still clearly wondering what this was all about.

"A couple months ago, I think, the lumber company's accountant recommended three books to read. These books described how a Communist or socialist ideology is able to take over governments of democratic countries. I want to give you these three books to read, but I don't want anybody else to know about it, okay."

"Okay. What are they?" he asked.

"*The New Class, Animal Farm,* and *The Church of Silence.* Man, you've got to read these books; the similarities between what was done during the Russian Revolution and the formation of the Iron Curtain after the end of World War II and what is going on here right now are uncanny!" I explained.

"Don't worry, I know what you mean," Evelio responded.

I paused to take a smoke. For a minute, we just kept on walking, and then I continued, "Well … there is something else I want to tell you. It is very important that you don't tell anyone. I'm counting on you." I took a drag of my smoke. "You know how things are changing in this country, and you know that I don't like what is going on. And I know that you don't either. You can't say anything against these people. I thought they claimed that this is a democracy, yet you can't have an opinion against them. We don't have brothels anymore, all the old newspapers are gone, and Radio Kramer is gone. We are being bombarded with revolutionary propaganda day and night. See these cigarettes we are smoking; they are going to disappear very soon. This is a mess," I said.

"Yeah, I know …," Evelio replied slowly, "so … what do you have in mind? What are you going to do?" he asked.

"I believe that I'll be leaving Cuba very soon," I said.

"But … how? When?" he asked.

"Okay, this is how I think it's going to happen. My father's brother works for a shipping company, Garcia Line. My father is going to speak with my uncle to see if he can get me a job there. If he can, then I'm gone!" I responded.

"Wow … so … when is this going to happen?" Evelio inquired.

"Soon, I guess. He just made port a couple of days ago; I think my father is going to talk to him tomorrow."

"Let's say that you can get the job with Garcia Line. Then what are you going to do after that? After all, Castro may eventually also confiscate Garcia Line, just like many others so far. Then you are stuck again, right?" Evelio asked.

"Yeah I know that possibility exists. I'm contemplating asking for asylum in the United States if it's possible. I don't know. I have to see how it goes, you know," I responded.

For a moment, we shared a silence.

"Well, let's make way our back home," I suggested. "I'm going to bring you the books tomorrow. I don't want to give them to you in front of Lasi. Remember, not a word to anybody."

"My lips are sealed," Evelio responded.

What could my future look in a Socialist-Communist Cuba? Well, it did not look too good to me, at this point. I hoped that getting the job with Garcia Line would be, for me, an opportunity to seek a way out.

Chapter 8

My Merchant Marine Card and Something Extra

My uncle Enrique had managed to get me a job on board the SS *Houston*.[1] A position as an oiler was open in the engine room. My job consisted of applying lubricants of different grades to working parts of the engine and supporting machinery and equipment. I did not care what it was, as long as I could get out of Cuba.

My uncle told me that there was a little wrinkle in this whole plan—in order to work on the ship, I had to have a merchant marine license and get a Cuban passport to leave the country. He told me to get moving and get it all done as soon as possible. I was now left to deal with the suspicion of others—suspicion that I was trying to leave Cuba and turning my back on a glorious revolution—and to beat the growing Cuban socialist bureaucracy.

My uncle Enrique circa 1970

I went to the Cuban Port Authority to apply for my merchant permit. I do not recall the official name of this facility. I logged in my name on the waiting list and joined the others in waiting.

67

A very nice-looking woman would come out of an office and call people from the list. There must to have been about four or five of us.

My turn finally came up, and she asked me to enter her office.

"Good morning," she greeted.

"Good morning," I responded in kind.

"My name is Dulce, and you are …?" she said, smilingly.

"My name is Desiderio Sanchez. You may call me Desi, for short."

"Have a seat. I am the port's captain secretary. What is your business here today?" she asked me politely, while she was seated behind her desk.

"Thank you. Well, this is my first time here; I do not know what to do. I have an opportunity to work as a merchant marine for the Garcia Line. My uncle told me to come here and ah … What do I have to do?" I said, hoping that the information was not going to be too complicated, as government things tend to be.

"Okay, well, you have to do a few things. First, you need a passport. Do you have one?" Dulce asked me with a routine sounding voice. I was sure she explained the answers to the same questions all day long.

"No," I responded.

"Next, you need to apply for a merchant marine permit," she continued.

"Ah … well … that sounds easy," I said with some relief in my voice.

She turned around and opened one of the drawers from the cabinet behind her and handed me several forms.

"Here. Fill out these forms. To get your permit, you also need to pass the merchant marine exam."

"How much time are we talking about for taking the exam?" I was a little concerned now. I knew this was going to get complicated.

"This is the process," Dulce explained, her instructions very precise. "You need to study for the exam. We put your application on the pile, and then, when your name comes up, we will call you to schedule you for the actual test and pass the exam. The port captain has to review your test, and if you pass, he'll sign on it. You will get a card with your picture on it. We are talking about days, maybe weeks, and in some cases, a whole month."

"Oh no, I don't think I have that much time!" I put my hands on my face; I think I looked very panicky.

"What do you mean? What seems to be the problem?" She asked me with a tone of concern and curiosity at the same time.

I took a deep breath. "Okay, here is my predicament—my uncle works for the Garcia Line. His ship, the *Houston*, is in port for repairs. He told me that the crew may be here for only two weeks, maybe three tops. Then they will go, whether I'm ready or not. I don't want to miss this ship!" I explained to her, rather nervously.

She looked into my eyes very quietly for a few moments. She turned around again and took what looked like a small book from one of the cabinets against the wall.

"Well ... that is the process. I'm going to give you this manual. Study it hard! Do you have a phone where I can get in touch with you?" she said, showing her willingness to help me but within her limitations.

"Well, I don't have a telephone at home, but you can call me at work from 7:00 a.m. to 4:00 p.m. Is that okay?"

"That's fine. I will call you and let you know about the test. Meanwhile, get moving with your passport," she said.

"Thank you. Thank you!" I said, shaking her hands in gratitude.

I left the merchant marine office feeling very special and thinking that maybe Dulce would not do this much for everyone sitting out there in the waiting room.

I did everything—slept, ate, took showers, and went to the bathroom—with this manual in my hands, except while I was at work. I obviously did not want anyone to see what I was doing. My appointment to take the Cuban Merchant Marine exam was almost three weeks away. This was cutting it very close; it was precisely when the repairs for the SS *Houston* were to be completed. My application for a passport was moving along.

My next challenge was to get my passport as soon as possible. After our private conversation just a few days before, Evelio was also contemplating leaving the country. From that point on, he accompanied me on all of my business as I got all the needed paperwork in order. No one else knew of our intentions. Evelio and I stood together in line for several hours at the State Ministry, along with thousands of Cubans, also applying for their passports. Inside the ministry building, employees would not make the wait any easier for us; we filled out our applications and submitted the legal paperwork, such as our birth certificates.

About three days later, I did get a call on the lumber company phone from an employee from the State Ministry requesting me come back to the ministry again. When I went there, the ministry employees explained that, apparently, there was a person connected to the ousted Batista regime that had my same name (Desiderio.) It became apparent to the employees, once I was there in person, that I could not possibly be that individual, since I was a lot younger, our last names were not the same, and we resided in opposite sides of the country—bureaucratic stupidity?.

A couple of days after this call and my visit to the ministry, I received correspondence from the ministry that I could go to the building and get my passport. I now had my passport in hand.

The month of January 1961 was a very busy month for me. I had to do a lot of running around. Between the State Ministry, the port authority, Garcia Line, work, and study, I was stressed out.

One thing I wanted to do was to go to my school in old Havana and obtain a letter of recommendation from the rectory about my person and accomplishment at Saint Augustine, in the event that I was going to be able to ask for asylum in the United States. I did fail to ask for my grade records. As it turned out, this was just as well, since all my personal effects were lost on the *Houston*.

The lobby was cool, the school rectory was at my left, and to my right was the room prior to the entrance to the main altar, where I'd helped with Mass for so many years, and many fond memories came to my mind. I took a seat on one of the dark mahogany benches there, waiting to see either Father McKniff or Father Kennedy. My heart fell to the floor when Emilia walked in the door; she was the last person in the world I was expecting to see. She looked very distraught. I got up immediately and approached her with a warm embrace and a kiss on her cheek.

"What happened, Emilia? You look very upset. Is there anything I can do?" I asked her, truly concerned about her.

"I don't know. I'm here to see Father McKniff," Emilia responded, with a tone of urgency in her voice.

"Come here. Sit with me." I took her by her hand, and we sat together on the bench. "I'm here to see Father McKniff also. Tell me, what's going on?" I asked, looking into her eyes.

"I'm very upset. My boyfriend has been incarcerated because he was caught carrying weapons and compromising documents against Castro." Emilia's words rushed out of her mouth.

"I'm sorry to hear that. That is a very serious charge," I responded, concluding that, if there was any hope for me to be with Emilia, this revelation had shut me down totally.

"I'm hoping that Father McKniff and the church can help me to intercede on his behalf with the government and help him," she quickly explained.

"Don't worry about it. I'm sure that Father McKniff will be able to help your boyfriend," I said, knowing full well that her boyfriend was in very big trouble, and there was nothing anybody could do about it.

"I hope you're right, Desi," she said, her voice trembling.

"Look, here comes Father McKniff," I said as he showed up at his office door.

"Good morning, Father," we said in unison.

"Good morning, Emilia. Desi, haven't see you for a while," said Father McKniff. The father spoke fluent Spanish as well as Filipino.

"It has been hard for me to come down to the city ever since I moved to Santo Suarez, and I'm also busy working," I responded. "We are here to see you, Father. Emilia was here first," I conceded.

"Thank you, Desi." Emilia looked up at me with gratitude for ceding my turn to her.

Emilia did not ask me, and I did not tell her, my reason for being there. *I wish I could tell her of my feelings for her,* I thought. I was leaving Cuba soon, and I had a strong feeling that I was never going to see her again.

I had never been outwardly romantic, but music had always been an integral part of my personality. I always linked songs to important events in my life. As Emilia left with Father McKniff for her interview, a song came to my mind that would encompass my memory of Emilia—"You Don't Know Me", a country song sung by Jerry Vale in 1956. In 1962, Ray Charles recorded the song. This version, which is my favorite version, has to be the best.

You give your hand to me
And then you say, "Hello."

I concluded, at this point, that telling Emilia my feelings for her wouldn't matter; her only concern at the moment was the welfare of her boyfriend. All I could take with me was nice memories of her, of when I lived on the same street that she lived on.

Evelio and I still made time to have fun with our girlfriends, though we were winding down our visits with Maggie and Nena. We were meeting new girls in our neighborhood.

Around mid-January 1961, Lasi's younger brother, Chichi, had met two very attractive sisters, Lidia and Nadia. Lidia was fifteen, and Nadia was eighteen. He introduced us to them.

Our attention changed focus to those two; they were a lot of fun. In fact, I had already met Nadia when I was collecting union dues for the Barbers and Beauty Salons Union; she worked as hairdresser at an establishment in my Vedado zone, a small coincidence. Evelio and I started visiting the sisters very frequently, taking them out, as friends, to the movies and to nightclubs.

One Saturday night, February 25, Lidia and Nadia told their mother that they were going to spend the night at one of her girlfriend's home and wouldn't be back until about 8:00 a.m. the next morning; instead, they went out with us. Evelio and I took them clubbing to La Red (The Net). La Red was a very popular nightclub in Havana, located in La Rampa, El Vedado.

Picture taken at "La Red" February 25, 1961
From left to right; Desi, Lidia, Nadia and Evelio. This outing was an all nighters.

Recently, Lidia, Evelio's wife—they were married in 1965—showed me a forgotten picture taken at La Red that Saturday night.

We danced, drank, and talked, even when the nightclub had closed by 5:00 a.m. We could not take the girls home yet, so we all hopped on a bus, and toured the city for a good hour and a half. We then went for breakfast at one our favorite spots, La Wakamba, a big cafeteria in our neighborhood in Santo Suarez. La Wakamba was open by around six in the morning.

By the time we took Lidia and Nadia home, it was about eight o'clock in the morning. We talked for days about what a great time we'd had that evening. Eventually Lidia told her mom about their escapade with us. My last picture and outing with Lidia, Nadia, and Evelio was on March 12, 1961, at the Havana Zoo. A few weeks after that picture was taken, my life would change forever.

***

Visit to the Havana Zoo, March 12, 1961 From left to right; Evelio, Nadia, Lidia and Desi. Picture taken a few days before my departure from Cuba.

I was very fortunate that the SS *Houston* had to stay a little longer; an important part that was needed to complete the repair had not been received as of yet. I knew that the *Houston's* captain was growing impatient, due to logistics and schedule commitments. I surmised that the captain's mind-set was this—the minute the repairs are completed, I am out of here.

I think I am losing my hair, I thought.

I was still using every minute of my day to study the merchant marine manual. Evelio was helping me to study and memorize the manual. I was always on the lookout for the person in charge of the Comité para la Defensa de la Revolución in my own apartment building—he was always snooping into everything everyone did—and also for some of my friends and neighbors who were integrating into the revolution.

At work and at home, I went about my daily routine, except that now I was totally immersed in the merchant marine manual. About four days after having given me the manual, Dulce called me at work and asked me if I had any questions or needed help with my studies. I was shocked; she said that my test had been scheduled for the following day. It had been about six or seven days since I had applied for my permit. More surprisingly yet, she also gave me hints about the general subject of the test itself, just to make sure that I would pass. I told her not to worry. I knew the manual forward and backward.

I was usually at work between 7:00 and 7:30 a.m. I had gotten up extra early the day I had to take the merchant marine test, gone to the grocery store, and called work. Matias was not there yet, but I talked to Ariel, the other owner. Ariel was in charge of the company warehouse, "the floor." He and his crew were usually at work by 6:00 a.m. I told Ariel that I was going to be a little late for work that day.

I took the full hour allotted to complete the test; I went over the questions until I was satisfied that I had done the best I could. When I stepped out of the test room, Dulce asked me to come into her office and have a seat.

"So ... Tell me. How do you think you made out on the test?" she asked me with a curios look on her face.

"I am very confident that I came out on top. Maybe I had a little problem with one question, but I don't think it's going to hurt my score," I said, confident that I had done just fine.

"I'm very happy for you. If everything is okay, you will be called to pick up your merchant marine card in a couple of days," she told me.

"Fantastic!" I was happy.

Dulce lowered her voice; she made a move with her hand for me to come a little closer. "Do you know why your call for the test came up so quickly?" she whispered.

"Well ..." I hesitated. "I admit that I was very surprised. Why?" I asked.

"I moved your application up a little every day toward the top of the heap," she confessed. "Of course, this is not to be repeated to anyone. You do understand, right?"

Why did she do that? I do not know. I could only thank her profusely and tell her that I was praying that God would bless her beyond her dreams.

It was now way into the second week, when completion of the SS *Houston* repairs were to have been completed. *How close can I possibly cut it!*

Two days had passed since I'd taken my exam. I was excited. I was now on my way to pick up my merchant ID card at the port. I had given Ariel my early morning phone call about being a little late for work that morning.

"Mr. Sanchez, you did very well, one of our highest scores," the captain said, and he and Dulce shook my hand and presented me with my merchant marine card and the proper paperwork.

"Thanks," I responded, smiling, and glad that it was all over.

We exchanged a little pleasant talk between us and then shook hands again. Dulce said that she would walk me to the door, and I received another shocker! We shook hands again, and this time, she passed a small piece of paper on to me. Where in the world had she kept that little piece of paper? In her bra? I did not know. She looked intensely into my eyes (I always liked maintaining eye contact). And then she whispered, "Please call me."

When I got to work after coming back from the port, I told Matias that I needed to talk to him in private.

He said, "Wait until everyone goes home, and then we'll talk, okay?"

I had to wait to after 5:00 p.m., almost 6:00 until everyone had left. Meanwhile, I did some work to catch up for the time I lost during my test.

"Okay, Desi, what's going on?" Matias asked me to seat by his desk.

"Well, you know, we have talked occasionally about how things are going here with our new revolution. You have even mentioned, while fooling around, that this is a Communist-inspired revolution and that big changes are coming," I started my conversation.

"Yeah, I know I have said that. I know it sounded like I was ... But I wasn't really fooling around," he said in a serious tone.

"As you know, a couple of days ago I called and gave some excuse to take some time off. For that, I apologize to you. Let me explain why."

"Okay, go on," he said, looking for a more comfortable position in his chair.

"For the past several weeks, I have been studying to take the test and become a merchant marine. Today I got my merchant marine card. I recently got my passport, and also, I secured a job with a merchant line company," I went on.

"But," Matias fumbled for the words. "How ...? When ...? How did you get the job?" I think Matias was very surprised to hear this from me; to him, I did not seem the type to take all of these actions.

"My uncle works for the Garcia Line, and he got me a job on his ship. You know, I really owe you an apology; you are the last person on this planet that I would deceive, but I think that you understand why I had to keep this a secret. Life here is not getting any safer. I think that your company will eventually be confiscated by Castro's government. You can

75

see that Alfredo and a couple of other employees have joined the militia,"
I continued.

Matias, meanwhile, looked at me with amazement. "I know," he
eventually said. "I believe that you are right. I still can't quite get over
how quietly you did it all. You never gave anyone a hint. I can understand.
I think I would have done the same thing. Are you coming back at all?"
he asked me.

"I don't know, Matias. Garcia Line does shipping from Havana to the
United States and other ports around the Gulf. But how long is it going to
be before I come back to Havana? I don't know." I hesitated, and silence
hung between us before I said, "It could be a couple of months."

I added, "There is one detail that concerns me while I'm gone."

"And what is that?" asked Matias, lighting up a cigarette.

"My mother and sisters. My dad left home, and I've been helping
with the household. I don't know when I'm going to get paid from Garcia
Line. Neither do I know when I'm going to be able to send them money
in the beginning—you know, until I know how things work." I joined
Matias with a smoke. I smoked Winston cigarettes, my favorite American
brand. Ariel smoke Chesterfields. Matias smoked Cuban's cigarettes and
an occasional cigar.

"That may not be a problem. You know that you have vacation money
coming, right?" he said, after taking another puff.

"I do?" I did not recall us talking about vacation pay.

"Yeah, you do. Don't worry. This is what we are going to do. I want
you to sign several receipts for the money that you have coming from
your vacation. I'll give your mother and sisters the money as if it was you
salary," he explained.

"Okay, but how are you going to keep this from Alfredo's nose? Could
it be dangerous for you if he finds out?" I asked him.

"Don't worry about Alfredo. He is an idiot, and I'm the boss (at least
for now). I have my ways to handle the details. Tell your mother to come
at the end of the month that you leave, and I'll have your money ready
for her, okay?"[2]

I agreed, but I was still thinking about how he was going to do that.

"When are you leaving?"

"Well, that is the other little detail that I didn't tell you yet. My ship
is in repairs at the port. I start working this coming Sunday. The ship's

repairs are still in process. As soon as the ship's repairs are completed, I'm gone!" I said.

"Well ... Desi ... it was a pleasure to have you as my employee. My family and I, especially Elba, are going to miss you. I wish you good luck in your new job. I hope that, whatever you do, it will work out for you. And if you ever come back, please come down to see us, okay," he said, getting up from his chair and giving me a strong embrace.

I nodded in affirmation; I really could not say anything more. I believe that we both knew that we would never see each other again.

I had my private talk with Matias on a Wednesday, but I stayed at work until Friday so that I would not raise any suspicion. I told everybody that I was going be out for a few weeks due to a family emergency. Before I left the office, since I didn't have a phone of my own, I called the number written on that little piece of paper that Dulce had given me. She asked me to pay her a visit whenever I had some free time. I asked her if it was okay to come and see her that evening, and she said, "Yes!"

We agreed on about 9:00 p.m. I went home, took a shower, changed my clothes, and had dinner. I told my mother that I was going out with my friends and that I may be late. As I left, she said her usual, "Be careful."

Dulce lived in El Vedado—the same area that I'd worked during my stint with the Barbers and Beauty Salon Union. Her apartment was in a four-story white building, about two short blocks from La Rampa complex; the Malecon Boulevard was not too far away either. It was a bit after nine when I knocked at her door; I did not want to appear too anxious about whatever was going to happen, if anything was going to happen.

She opened the door. The apartment was modest but nice. There was a living room and dining area, separated by a couch. Across the couch were a TV and a record player on a nice stand. In a corner, a wheeled, metal cart served as a bar. On it were some liquor bottles, glasses, and an ice container. Several pictures on the wall depicted landscapes.

She opened the door and asked me to come in. She was dressed very casually. Her low-cut blouse showed some cleavage, nothing indecent but very sexy. She was not wearing high heels this time, just comfortable flats; she was about my height.

I realized, now that I was not under any stress, that she was really a very good-looking woman; her brown hair was picked up in ponytail. She looked younger than she had in the office. I think she was in her early thirties. She had nice, light brown/green eyes and not too round a face. She was wearing a little makeup; her lips, shaped kind of like a bow, were not too thick; her skin was neither too white nor too tan; and her body was very nice and curvaceous body, though not the body of the typical voluptuous Cuban woman.

I thought, *What could she possibly want to talk to me about?* I was all done with the exam.

"Hi, how are you?" I said while walking toward the center of the living room.

"Hi, come in. I am glad you were able to come. Here, sit down. Make yourself comfortable. Would you like something to eat?"

"Oh no, thank you. I had dinner earlier," I answered.

"Okay, how about something to drink? You can choose between Bacardi and Coca-Cola or VAT 69 and soda," she said while pointing at the bar-cart.

"I'll have VAT 69 and soda, thank you." I think I sounded a little nervous.

"Do you have to be that formal?" she asked.

"Well ... I don't know ..." I faltered, a little surprised. "I think I should show some respect. I'll try to behave."

"Did you have any trouble finding my place?" she asked while preparing the drinks. Her back was toward me, and I noticed that the back of her legs were very shapely.

"Oh no! I used to work around here about a year ago," I said.

"You did? You have to tell me about that. Do you mind if I play some music? I'll play nothing loud, just some nice instrumentals, I promise," she said, while looking for a record.

"No, I don't mind at all. I like that kind of music," I said, waiting to see what would develop from all this.

She brought my drink. She mixed a rum and Coca-Cola (Cuba Libre) for herself. We were sitting on the couch, turned to each other. I was keeping my distance. I took a sip of my drink and placed it on the living room stand in front of me.

"First, I ought to tell you that I'm not in the habit of bringing strangers or people I've just met to my apartment." She moved a little closer to me and took a sip from her drink.

"I ... ah ... didn't even think about that," I said, stuttering again.

"Then in that case, I consider your invitation a privilege and an honor ... Actually, I feel really special right now."

"Okay, don't butter me up. So ... tell me. How did it go today? How does it feel to be a bona fide merchant marine?" she asked.

"Well ... today I told my boss that I was leaving the lumber company and that this coming Sunday I would be starting to work with my uncle as a merchant marine. Lucky for me, the part the ship's captain was expecting to complete the repairs has not arrived yet. I can really use a breather after all the stress that I had these past few weeks." I took my glass and took another sip.

"I'm glad to hear that," she responded. "Tell me, was your boss surprised?"

"He definitely was. I don't think he expected to hear that news coming from me. My boss is a great person. He wished me the best," I said.

"I hope you don't mind if bring this up, but in your application, you mentioned that you graduated from an American school in accounting. You had a good job. I assume that you also know English. What made you want to become a merchant marine and get oily and dirty?" she asked inquisitively. She had another sip of her drink and waited for my answer.

"My uncle has been a merchant marine for many years. I thought that it would be a good experience for me at this time to see the world like he has. To me this is like ... an adventure. I can always come back to my accounting later on, if I don't like it. That is why I jumped at the opportunity," I explained.

She looked at me as if she did not quite believe my explanation. "I want to be honest with you. I helped you out because you gave me the impression that ... I thought ... that you were in some kind of trouble and needed to leave quickly," she said.

"You know ..." I faltered, not sure what to say. "It's very hard to trust anybody these days. I can only tell you that I am not in any kind of trouble, thus far."

She lowered her head a little, and then she said, "I know what you mean about trust."

"Dulce, look, I will always appreciate the chance that you may have taken in helping me out at your work. I'll never forget what you did for me; I'll never forget you for that matter. You were very perceptive in realizing that I was, for some reason, very nervous and stressed out. When I went to your office, I did not know what to expect. My uncle had told me that the repairs were going to be done very quickly. I thought that I had very little time to get ready and make it to the ship. I hope that you don't think that I took any advantage of you or misled you. The last thing on my mind was to think that anyone would help me get this done so quickly." I related to her my reasons for the office visit.

"I'm glad that you clarified your predicament to me. I understand that this is as far as you can go." She seemed to be glad that I was straight with her.

"Now, I have a question for you. Why does such a beautiful woman like you not have a boyfriend?

She was very quiet for a moment, as if she was contemplating what to say or whether to tell me that it was none of my business. She took another sip of her drink, seeming to want to take her time with an answer. She moved closer toward me and held my hand. "I think it has something to do with the word that you used a while ago—trust. I was married a few years back; it did not work out for me. I have a hard time trusting someone in that manner again. So here I am," she answered, opening her free hand toward my direction.

"I understand," I said.

We got very quiet for a few minutes. I do not how it happened. We just looked at each other, and before I knew it, we were kissing each other.

"I like you very much," she whispered in my ear.

Still holding hands, she and I stood up from the couch, and she led me to her bedroom. That night, I tried my very best to show her my gratitude, several times.

Out of everyone she may have been in contact with, why did she invite me to her apartment? Why did she make love to me? I could only surmise that I was a safe pick. Somehow, she knew that I was not coming back, so what could she possibly lose?

As for me, I had my merchant marine card in my pocket and something extra—more than I'd expected.

Chapter 9

Bye-Bye, Havana

Sunday—I believe it was about the first full week of March 1961—came; I had just celebrated my twenty-second birthday. I went to work on board the ship for the first time. My uncle introduced me to the captain, a jolly-looking, possibly Irish fellow in his early fifties—I cannot recall his name to save my life—and the crew on board. Jose R. and Angel G. were both ordinary-looking; I cannot recall much more about them. They were my oiler counterparts.

Miguel was one of our helmsmen. I do not know who the other helmsman was. Miguel was a bit older than me but the youngest of the rest of the crew, and about my height. He had tanned skinned and brown hair and was a very quiet person.

Julio, the quartermaster, was very nice and friendly. He respected authority and was willing to help. With dark skin and short, black hair, he looked to be in his early forties. He was very knowledgeable in his job. Julio was a Spaniard; I do not think that he was a Cuban citizen.

Arnold M. and Raimundo G., the boiler men, seemed to be in their thirties, They were both a bit heavy, maybe from too much beer; friendly; and a little crazy. They seemed to be good friends.

Jose G. was the second engineer. I didn't know much about Jose. He was obviously knowledgeable in his profession, and I believed that he had just joined the crew. He was a wiry-looking guy, a little taller than me, with a sculptured face and curly, black hair. He was maybe in his early forties.

Lucio S., my uncle's right-hand man, was the machine room assistant. He must have been very good; my uncle was a nice guy, but he was very demanding. Lucio was taller than me, had a medium complexion, and seemed to be in his early fifties. He was friendly and willing to help.

I was very excited about this whole business; I thought of it as an adventure. Little did I know, I would get more than I had bargained for.

We were at port, and the ship was still under repairs. Every day, for several days, at the end of my working shift, my boss, Uncle Enrique, would release me from my duties and send me home. It was on March 20 at the end of my workday that my uncle told me that the following day was going to be our last day in Havana. With all the repairs now completed, we were ready to sail first thing on the morning of March 21.

Enrique also said that I could not go home that evening. Potentially every day at the *Houston* could have been our departure day. From the first day I started working at the *Houston*, I had brought all my new working clothes and personal items on board and kept them in my cabin, not knowing when the day of my departure from the Havana port would be. There was no reason for me to go back home, other than to say a final farewell to my family. Of course, we had our final farewell every morning when I left home for the port. I stayed on board and went to sleep.

On March 21, a side-by-side motion awakened me; I heard a whistle blowing. I got dressed very quickly and went up on deck. It was a beautiful morning. On my right, the iconic Morro Castle guarded the entrance to the bay. To my left, were the predominantly colonial and Art Deco buildings of Old Havana, including Iglesia de Santo Angel (the Church of St. Angel), where I was baptized as a child. Among these were the parks, with their almond, laurel, royal Poinciana, coconut, and palm trees. As a child, I had flown kites at one of these parks. There stood the amphitheater, where the army, navy, and police bands played concerts during weekends, while the traditional evening cañonazo de las nueve (nine o'clock canon shot) fired from a canon in the Fortaleza de la Cabaña (Cabana Fortress) across the Havana Harbor entrance. The presidential palace stood tall, and the beautiful boulevards—El Paseo del Prado (El Prado Boulevard)[1] and El Malecon, which ran along the Havana seashore were prominent. There were the Hotel Nacional, the American Embassy building, the Maine Memorial, the Jewish Temple, La Rampa,[2] and the

FOCSA building.[3] I said to myself, *Take a good look at this view and save it in your memory. You may never see this again!*

My last view of Havana from the Houston, March 1961.

I reflected as this view absorbed me. I had just turned twenty-two; I was doing a strange job; and except for my uncle, I did not know anybody. *Where am I really going?* I asked myself. *How and where am I going to jump ship?*

My uncle and I had not discussed the topic of jumping ship, but I believe he had also had this thought. Enrique had confided to me that there was a suspicion among the officers of the ship that Castro had infiltrated a couple of his agents within our group as crew members. That meant that we must refrain from discussing politics. Besides myself, two other new crew members were on board; the officers thought that at least one of them was the spy. I figured that my uncle and I would talk about jumping ship when the right time came.

I regretted one thing at that time—other than my architectural drafting manual, I had forgotten to bring a good supply of books. Life on board the ship was easygoing but boring—a drastic change from Havana and my escapades there.

It was time to make my rounds again. Every other hour, I had to climb up a small staircase to reach the top of the engine cylinders. There, I put some gooey lubricant in cups that led to the engine cylinders. I had to be careful since they were very hot. Once I was done with the engine cylinders, I had to attend to the several pumps that needed lubrication all the time. Finally, I went down the tunnel and lubricated the turning axle;

into receptacles spaced every so many feet apart, I placed a different grade of lubricant. At the end of the tunnel, stairs led to the deck.

I took several breaths of fresh air before going back to that hot hellhole that was the engine room. Stopping by the kitchen to see if there was something cool to drink, I found only water, which would do. Downstairs, Enrique was minding his command post. I worked with my uncle during my four-hour morning shift; you would think that this was the right place to talk about my plans to jump ship, but not really. First, the ship's engine noise was right next to us, and we were also surrounded by noisy pumps. You had to shout so that the person next to you could hear you.

The rest of the engine room's crew would take turns sitting by a couple of bar stools and a small, tall table, cooled off by an overhead duct with a fan that brought fresh air from the outside. The engine room was a very hot place.

The ship's cook was not that great, but it was not as if you could go out and get another choice of cuisine. I made the best of it. After lunch, I would go on deck and enjoy the breeze. Being in the middle of the ocean was weird; you look around in a 360-degree turn, and it feels like you're sitting in a round soup dish.

At about 4:00 p.m., just before dinnertime, I would take a shower and get dressed. I would wear a nice turtleneck and my new grey Wrangler jeans that I had bought at Sears. Every day when my crew mates saw me freshly bathed and wearing clean clothes, they would ask me the same question:

"Where are you going tonight?"

"Get out of here," I would respond.

Sleeping quarters were not that great either. I bunked with the other oilier, Angel G., in a very small cabin at the stern of the ship—my bouncing room, as I referred to it. In the beginning, it was very hard to sleep. The ship would jump up and down and sideways; a clanking noise, as if somebody was awake and hammering against the ship's wall, sounded all night. The cabin was hot, but nothing neared the heat of the engine room. This was going to take some getting used to it. Eventually—I do not how it happened—I did not hear the noise anymore. I was so tired from the heat of the engine room and the work that I would simply fall asleep, noise and all. I guess I was getting used to the banging and jumping.

My second shift was with the second engineer in command, Jose. Jose didn't say much, but I suspected, as he related to me that he had moved from Spain to Cuba recently, that he was illegal. I did not attempt a lot of conversation with him either. As usual, at the end of my night shift, I went to sleep in my noisy cabin; wiped out from the heat of the engine, I was soon asleep.

The whole routine started all over again the next day.

Sometimes, after supper, I would knock at my uncle's cabin to catch up, just family talk. We had not seen each other much before I'd started working with him.

One time, the conversation turned to a subject that had been on my mind for a while.

"May I come in, uncle?" I knocked on the open door cabin.

"It's open!" he answered.

"How are you doing?" I asked him as I sat at a nearby chair.

"Good. Are you getting used to sea life?" he asked me.

"Yeah, it's different, but I think I'll be okay."

"How are your mom and sisters doing?" my uncle asked me after taking a puff at his cigarette.

I lit one myself. "I want you to know I never smoked in front of my father," I told him before answering his question. "They're doing okay, considering the circumstances. I was able to arrange with the lumber company for them to collect some vacation money I had coming. I hope that will be okay until I can send them some money.

"You know, I talked to you more than I talked to my father," I added after taking a smoking pause.

"Why is that?" he asked, looking at me rather inquisitively.

"I don't know, but it seems that it came to a point that he didn't know what was going on in my life, it just seems that I could not make friends with him, or maybe he couldn't make friends with me. I never really held a conversation with him that I can recall, not like I do with you."

"Well," my uncle exclaimed.

"Look, I'll give you a good example. When I turned nineteen, my father told me that he wanted to have a private talk with me. Of course, I thought, what did I do now? He started by telling me that I was of the age to know a few facts about life, you know the birds and the bees, how babies are made, and all that kind of stuff. I let him talk for a few minutes, and then I told him that I had been with women and had been having sex since I was sixteen and that there was not a lot he could tell me about that subject, 'I think you are a little late,' I told him."

"Hmm," my uncle exclaimed.

"I felt pretty bad after a while, that I had cut him off that way. But I was still pretty upset after what he did to my mother on New Year's Day," I said.

"Yeah I know. I don't know what got into him. However, maybe he and your mother could not get along anymore," my uncle replied. "I'm not making any excuses for him," he added quickly. "Divorce is something that has to be very hard on everyone in the family."

"Did you know that my sister Inez got pictures of Adelfa kissing and in the arms of another man?" I asked.

"No. How did she do that?" my uncle asked me.

"She hired a private investigator; he followed her for several days and took lots of pictures."

"She has always been something," my uncle remarked. "So what happened?"

"She took all the pictures to Lamas and showed them to Adelfa and everyone around her."

"Did my brother see them?" my uncle asked.

"I don't know. This is a mystery to me. I don't understand. A lot of people saw the pictures; at the very least, there must have been rumors around him about it. You know how people's gossiping gets around, especially around work. Apparently, it was not enough for him; the fact is that he is still with her."

My uncle did not answer; we both took a drag from our cigarettes.

After a short pause I said, "Did you know that he hit my mother for the first time in one of their arguments?"

"No," my uncle answered slowly. "I … didn't know."

"I was not there at the time, but when he came to visit Zonia, I told him that if he ever hit my mother again, I would get a bat and I would hit him with it when he least expected it. I felt pretty bad about saying that to my own father afterward."

"Hmm."

"I'm sorry. I don't think that I should have brought up this topic, but I guess I needed to tell you. I have not talked about this with anybody."

As far as the topic that I wanted to talk about, the question of jumping ship, that was left for another day. I decided that I would wait until I knew where we were going first before I discussed the matter with Enrique. I am sure that he did not want to talk about the same thing every night and have it become an obsession.

I do not remember exactly why it happened, but for the next few days, my uncle and I did not feel like talking about anything heavy or important, so we just talked about things of the day. It had been over two weeks since we'd left Cuba to … who knew where the hell we were going. It just seemed to me that we were going around in circles in the Gulf, a "Cruise to Nowhere."

The following day, we woke up to a stormy day. The sea was rough, and the ship was jumping. The sailors told me that it was not a big deal; this storm was nothing compared to the ones that they had encounter in the past. "If the ship had any cargo, it would have been better for you," one commented.

At my breakfast time, I did not eat too much. I did not want to get my stomach sick, and it was feeling sort of queasy. This time, as I went to my morning shift, I had to hold on to whatever I could grab on my way down to the engine room. Since the engine room was in the middle of the ship, the jumping was not as bad. My uncle was already at the air station smoking his morning cigarette. Before I left for lunch break, my uncle reminded me not to drink many liquids. I did not have a big lunch either. I stayed in the kitchen area most of the time after lunch, shooting the breeze with the guys; it was definitely more comfortable in the middle of the ship.

I had my afternoon shower, as usual, and I wore clean clothes but did not get "dressed up" this time, saving myself a "Where are you going tonight?" I just did not feel like "getting dressed." I had had my supper about five thirty that afternoon. As usual, I was at my post at 8:00 p.m. I felt that the food in my stomach was not going anywhere, and I had swallowed a stone. I would try my best not think about it.

The second half of my shift was at 10:00 p.m. It was my turn to use all of the lubricants again, starting with the engine lubricating cups. The storm seemed to have picked up a bit, and it was difficult to get around. I went stumbling about, lubricating the rest of the equipment and pumps. By the time I reached the tunnel to do the axle lubrication, I was not feeling good at all. By the time I'd completed lubricating the axle, I knew I was going to heave my supper. It was not easy to hold on, and as I went up the vertical ladder from the tunnel to the deck, I thought, *Go sailing, see the world, have a good time.* The ship was moving up and down and sideways.

Somehow, I made it to the deck; the rancid smell of the lubricant remained in my nose and throat. It was dark and windy, the sky looked like purple, and lightning broke the darkness all around me. Waves pounded on the old ship, reaching deck. I had to hold on to whatever I found nearby. No one else was on deck but me; it would have taken a little while, to say the least, for the rest of the crew to figure out that I had gone overboard.

Had I looked at myself in a mirror, I'm sure I would have looked very green. I finally heaved my supper overboard, while being hit by the waves coming over the deck. It took me a few minutes to get back in shape. Fighting the winds, I finally made it to the kitchen.

Lucio and Miguel were there.

"What the hell happened to you?"

"Why are you so wet? Your face looks very green."

They laughed and pointed at me as they asked these questions.

Of course, I did not think that my condition was funny at all. I told them what had just happened to me.

Lucio went to the cupboard, pulled out a package of saltine crackers, and handed it to me. "Here, eat these. It will help you get your stomach back inside."

I took the soda crackers and started eating them. Lucio and Miguel were still laughing at me.

I went back to the engine room. "You got sick in the storm, eh?" said Jose, looking at the package of soda crackers in my hand.

"It's a long story," I said and continued with my work.

It did not take long to get dried up. I could not wait to finish my shift, go to my cabin, and go to sleep.

The next morning, I felt much better but did not have much of a breakfast. My stomach still felt uneasy. The ship was not moving as much as the previous day. Or was it that I was getting used to it?

I never dined with my uncle Enrique; he dined at the officer's mess hall.

I went down to the engine room and started my shift as usual. My uncle was smoking his cigarette by the cooling station under the fan. I told him about my ordeal of the previous night.

As I walked away to start my first round, my uncle said, "Welcome to the SS *Houston*, sobrino!"

Chapter 10

A Great Time in New Orleans?

We had been at sea for about seventeen days. I woke up asking myself the same question I'd been asking for quite some time, *When are we going to know where we are going?* Given the amount of time we had been navigating, I figured we must be approaching Europe!

Figuring, I'd better get going, I made my way to the mess hall. After breakfast, I headed down the stairs. My uncle was already in the engine room, smoking his morning cigarette and sitting on one of the high chairs under the air vent.

"Good morning, sobrino.[1] How are you doing?" my uncle greeted me.

"Good morning, tío,"[2] I responded routinely. "I don't know; I slept as usual with the banging noise at stern."

"Guess what? I have some news for you about where we are going," he said, lightly banging his hand on our working table by the air duct.

That woke me up. "Finally, I thought, until now, that we were just going around and around in circles. I'm almost sure I saw the same seagull fly by several times," I joked. "So ... where are we going?" I added with anticipation.

"You are going to love it; we are going to New Orleans to pick up a load," he told me.

"Great! I'm assuming you have been there before," I said.

"Every time we've gone there, we've had a great time. I'm sure the guys will tell you," he said, smiling.

"How long are we going to be there? Are we going to be able to go to town? See the world? Maybe make some decisions?" I replied, trying to get more information.

"Whoa! Now you want to know more. I do not know anything beyond what I just told you. We will find out as soon as we get there, okay?" he responded.

The SS Houston on the way to New Orleans.
(Courtesy of B.O.P. Veterans Association Brigade 2506.)

I was excited. *Is this where we are going to jump ship? I thought. What if the authorities do not let us in?* I didn't want to bring up the issue now, but if anybody knew what to do, it would have to be my uncle. *I am sure he will let me know when the time comes,* I assured myself. So I thought.

During dinner, Lucio, Miguel, and I were very excited about calling port at New Orleans. Apparently, as my uncle had told me, this would not be their first visit to the city.

"My uncle tells me that you guys have been to New Orleans before," I said anxiously. "Come on, tell me about it."

"Okay," said Lucio, trying to draw me a mental picture. "New Orleans is a fun town, but most of the action is in two main streets—Bourbon Street and Canal Street."

"What's in these two streets?" I asked.

"There are many bars and clubs. During Mardi Grass, which by the way, we missed, tons of people party, lots of women from everywhere," Miguel said.

"Mardi Grass? What's Mardi Grass?" I'd never heard of it before.

"Mardi Grass is like the Carnival[3] festivities in Havana, just a little bit wilder."

"This block party, if you want to call it that, revolves around the New Orleans center streets such as Bourbon Street."

Lucio and Miguel were talking at the same time, vying to be the one with the best explanation.

"Some clubs even have shows where women take off their clothes right in front of you!" Miguel added, putting his hands on my shoulders and shaking me.

"You're kidding me!" I opened my eyes wide.

"You may even 'get lucky,'" said Lucio, winking.

"Get lucky? What do you mean by that?" I asked him, thinking that I was going to participate in some kind of game.

Lucio made an obscene gesture with his hands and lower body.

"Oh … I get it. Okay … I'm ready!" I said.

I still could not believe my luck; I had thought that we might be going to Mexico or other places in Central and South America.

While everyone continued with his own stories about New Orleans, I remembered a conversation that I'd had several months ago with my friend Rodi before my decision to leave Cuba and before the opportunity to work with the Garcia Line had presented itself.

"Hi, Rodi, haven't seen you for awhile. Are you still hanging out at Mirtha's home?" I asked him. Mirtha was his girlfriend at the time, and she became his wife a couple of years later.

"Yeah, you know." He shrugged his shoulders.

"Man, you don't go out with us anymore. I haven't seen your brother, Emilio, for quite some time now. Is he working nights?" I said, sounding like I was complaining.

Rodi paused for a minute and lowered his voice. He moved a little closer to me, as if he was about to tell me a secret. "Well, he left for New Haven, Connecticut, about a month ago."

I looked at him very surprised and asked, "You're kidding! What's in New Haven?"

"My mother's cousin and his wife have been living there for a few years. They have good jobs and a house, so they told Emilio. They even had a job ready for him when he got there," he explained, still in a low voice.

"Oh my God. I didn't know your brother was in the US. No wonder I haven't seen him for a while. You know this is really a coincidence; I'm also somewhat connected to New Haven. Do you remember when I belonged to the Columbian Squires? One of my jobs in the squires was as a notary. I communicated frequently with the squires' main office, in New Haven. In fact, it is the headquarters for the Knights of Columbus. I made some connections there, but I am not sure if they can help me.

"Just between you and me," I added, "I would like to go to the US, but I don't see how at this point. I would think that you and your family will follow Emilio, right?" I said amazed at the coincidence that New Haven was a focal point of both his and my connections.

"Yeah, I think," he responded hesitantly. "But I don't know when ... Yeah, I think eventually." He didn't sound too sure about how future events may develop.

From that point on, Rodi and I fantasized a little about going to New Haven, Connecticut, and getting out of Cuba before it went down in the dumps. Going to New Haven, at that time, had been a very far away and kind of unrealistic dream for me.

I thought about that conversation with Rodi, now that I was on my way to New Orleans. I was getting closer to my goal of freedom from Socialist-Communism and the promise of a decent life again.

During supper and before my second shift, the conversation still revolved around New Orleans. We seemed to have a one-track mind—women, drinking, and women.

It was soon time for me to go back to my evening shift, hoping that tomorrow would come as quickly as possible. While I was oiling the cups in the axle's tunnel (great acoustics), my mind wandered again to New Orleans. A great song from another one of my favorite's singers, Fats Domino, came to mind, and I started singing:

I found my thrill
On Blueberry Hill
On Blueberry Hill
When I found you ...

The following morning, on my way to eat breakfast, I was looking yonder to see if I would see anything other than 360 degrees of sea around me. After lunch, I took a little walk around and went up on deck to get some fresh air. For the first time, I saw several dolphins happily swimming, jumping over our waves, and playing along the ship's bow. Later on, I saw the US coast for the first time. A funny feeling of anticipation came over me as we made our approach. I noticed a big installation and a sign above it that read "Domino Sugar Refinery." I figured that this was one of the largest sugar producers. I couldn't wait to get off this bucket and get to know New Orleans.

We finally anchored. *But where are we?* I did not see the same landscape that I'd seen as we'd approached the bay. *When can we get off?*

As the chief engineer and second in command after the captain, my uncle was very busy at this time, so I could not ask him any questions.

The time to do my shift had come, so I went down to the engine room and started working. I had this nagging question—*Why are there so many military people and so much military equipment offshore?* And why, I wondered, did I have this creepy feeling in my stomach? I would find out later.

I did not work with my uncle during my morning shift, so I could not find out what was going on. I tried to find out through Jose, Angel, or Lucio, but they did not know anything either. They did tell me that we were definitely anchored at a military base, though they did not know why or for how long. I did not know where my uncle was. Besides, I liked to keep my place and not take advantage of my relationship. I just want to be like everyone else.

Okay, I concluded, *I guess I have no choice but to wait for the next morning to get more info.* For now, I was concentrating on working my worries away and planning to have a great time in New Orleans.

Chapter 11

Choosing between Life and Death

We anchored at dusk somewhere in New Orleans about April 7. I'm not sure exactly when; I wasn't taking notes at that time. First thing the morning following the day after our arrival, the captain requested that we meet on deck. I do not remember if I had breakfast or not, I think I did. I thought that this was how we got ready to go ashore, but I said to myself, *On a military base?*

The first of many shocks that I was to experience started with the announcement that we had to surrender our passports to the captain and that we could not get off the ship. *Okay, I thought, don't get alarmed. It's logical that they would not want civilians on a military base, and to make sure that no one does try to go ashore, they would take our passport as insurance.* I figured that, as soon as we had loaded whatever it was that we had to load, we would be out of the base and heading to Bourbon Street.

As usual, I had to report for my shift, but I did not stay long, since most of the machines and pumps were not operational now. After an hour or so, I went up on deck.

The deck was like a beehive of activity. The winches were busy loading speedboats on deck. Up the ramp came crates, big boxes, and fuel drums. Military people were busy and about, talking and giving commands. Occasionally, I heard someone giving orders in Spanish; it sounded funny when everyone else was speaking English. I saw crews soldering some contraptions at the port and starboard side, the bow and stern of the ship.[1] I concluded that all this activity was more than just loading materials.

I finally caught up with my uncle, and I asked him if he knew when we were leaving port and where we were going to unload this cargo. He said that it was going to be somewhere in Central America. I guess there would be no Canal Street, no liquor, no women, no good food, no good times, and no fun for me. The jumping ship idea was not looking too good at this point; Central America was not among my choices.

For now, all I could do was stand against the ship's railing on deck and try to look beyond the base grounds—beyond the buildings, the access roads, and my dream of getting out of this boat and starting a new life in freedom.

Things begin to unfold a couple of mornings later after my uncle and I had greeted each other and were commencing our shift. We did not have a lot to do, since we weren't moving, but there was some equipment that had to be maintained.

About an hour had elapsed, and we were all summoned to gather on deck so that we could hear a special announcement. I thought, *Now what?*

My uncle and I looked at each other, rather puzzled. We made our way on deck. Most everyone was already there. We heard a constant murmur, and we were all asking ourselves what the announcement could be.

A casually but well-dressed man was standing at the captain's bridge. He introduced himself as one the owners of Garcia Line Corp. I think his name was Eduardo Garcia, but I am not sure because of my problem with remembering names. He started with the normal, "You are all doing a great job ..." And then he dropped the *bomb*! I am paraphrasing:

"We have been chosen and given the opportunity to take a place in history. We are to take part in a plan to free Cuba of a man, Castro, who wants to take our country along a Communist path ..."

Then a man in a military uniform climbed up the bridge and introduced himself as Luis Morse. He spoke to us in Spanish. I would learn later that he was a Cuban Brigade commander and that he had replaced our ship's captain.

Luis Morse started by relating that this ships and others were part of an invading force and that we all had the task of bringing all this material to Nicaragua. In Nicaragua, we would meet a group of Cuban patriots, a brigade, that had been training hard and that would fight to free Cuba from the hands of Castro and his comrades. "Viva Cuba libre!" he shouted. (Long live free Cuba!) "Viva Cuba Libre!"

"Down with Castro!" everyone responded.

At the end of the patriotic harangue, Captain Morse also gave us a couple of choices to make; we could decide not to join the invading force, but for matters of security, those who decided not to participate would remain in a Nicaraguan detention center until the operation was over, at which point they would be repatriated. The others would become part of a group of patriots who would liberate Cuba from the hands of Communism. We had until the following day to make our choices.[2]

Needless to say, this was a scary proposition. I had never been exposed to a choice like the one given by Captain Morse. Until this morning, my biggest choices had been between wearing one color suit or another, a beer or a Canadian Club and soda (my favorite) in a nightclub, or the brunette or the blonde in a bordello. Decisions, decisions!

My mind was running away with all kind of thoughts. *What the hell am I going to be doing in a Nicaraguan jail anyway?*

What in the world have I gotten myself into?

What if the invading force loses the battle and I am left dead and forgotten there?

Wouldn't I stand out as a Castro sympathizer by not going?

What if we win? What if I am captured and sent to el Che's wall?

Being a hero was not in my original agenda. Dying in the service for an ideal or to save my country was a prospect to which I had not devoted a lot of thought at this point in my life.

I looked at my uncle and said, "It is time for us to have a serious conversation."

"Come to my cabin," he replied.

We sat, and I opened our conversation, not waiting for my uncle to open his mouth. "Okay, the way I see it, you don't know anybody in Nicaragua; I don't know anybody in Nicaragua. I'm not crazy about the idea of being placed under detention and giving everyone the impression that I support Castro. If the brigade wins, then I am not going to be in a good position. If they lose ... well, I'm going to be sent back to Cuba anyway, back to the nightmare that I wanted to leave behind." I am not sure, but I might have said all that in one breath. I took a deep breath and then asked, "So what do you think about all of this?"

"I'm ... ah ... I'm trying to digest all this, just like you. But it seems that I'm going to have to go. Look, I am the first engineer of this ship. This is my job. And I don't think I'm taking the Nicaragua option," he said thoughtfully.

"Yeah I agree … I know. But this is not your everyday merchant ship delivery job; we are going to be in the middle of a war!" I exclaimed.

"Well, Captain Morse has assured me that our job is limited to unloading the boats of supplies and men under the cover of night, and we'll be out of there before dawn," he explained. "Besides," he continued, "I hope you realize that, if we come out of this without getting killed and we do not overthrow Castro, we can never go back to our country. I am assuming that we will end up in the United States."

"I am going to go with you," I told him. "By the way, is there a plan B?"[3]

"A plan B? What do you mean by a plan B?" he asked, opening his hands.

"Yeah, you know, like … uh … suppose we don't finish unloading on time. After all, we are going there … to Cuba, then what?" I responded.

My uncle didn't say anything for a minute. Then he replied simply, "I guess that is a chance that we'll have to take."

"That tells me that there is no plan B. You know, Tío, I didn't talk with you about this very often, but you are aware that my intention has always been to jump ship, preferably in the States, and ask for political asylum. As you know, I know the language, I have my accounting degree from an American college, and I don't want to go back to Cuba. If I do, I know I'm going to get killed sooner or later," I said.

"Yeah, I know … I know that's what you want. Look, we just have to wait for the right moment. Obviously, we just can't do it now; we would be treated as deserters," he said.

"Okay," I agreed hesitantly. "I know … So what else did they tell you?"

"We are going to a place in Nicaragua called Puerto Cabezas," he responded.

I got up and walked toward the door. Just before I opened it, I turned around and looked at my uncle. "Okay, Puerto Cabezas it is," I said. "You know what? I don't have a warm and fuzzy feeling about this whole thing. See you later."[4]

Chapter 12

Right behind My Back

Okay, time out! I believe that now is an appropriate time to bring up a little background about what was going on in the US government during the Eisenhower and Kennedy administrations, while I was sweating it out in Havana—during 1960 and early 1961.

Let me briefly recount what was going on in my neighborhood, I was dealing with the Committee for the Revolution Defense person in my apartment building. At work, I was trying hard not to join the militia and, at the same time, selling and buying counterrevolutionary bonds. I was studying to become a merchant marine so that I could leave Cuba, and now I was sitting in a New Orleans military port without being able to get off the ship and go enjoy myself in Canal Street or Bourbon Street! Wasn't this a bummer?

During the remaining year of President Eisenhower's presidency, the CIA was busy preparing a plan to invade Cuba and recruiting Cuban exiles to what eventually became the Assault Brigade 2506. Composed of honest and reputable Cuban politicians and exiled Cubans citizens with a known history of not having been aligned with the Batista government—what a job! It was like trying to find a clean politician.

The plan called to organize a government in a free Cuba after Castro. I am not going to bored anybody, including myself, with all kind of numbers, details, and statistics or bickering among the CIA officials, the military, the president's people, or anyone else in the government who wanted to get credit for a successful campaign against the Castro regime at that time.

I believe that Washington knew, by early 1960, that Castro's revolution was Communist inspired and also that Washington realized that that the Soviet Union saw an opportunity here to expand its influence in Latin America. I also believe that a lot of very mad CEOs of the American companies and interest nationalized by Castro pressured Washington and wanted something to be done about Castro, especially since Castro had not paid back a single penny of the value of the nationalized (stolen by the Castro regime) American companies.

The final plan drawn by the CIA under the Eisenhower administration was evaluated by the Joint Chiefs of Staff, and from a military aspect, they concluded that a landing by a Cuban anti-Castro force had a fair chance of succeeding. The overall original plan to solve Cuba's Castro issue, based on what I read, was designed to win!

Using phony front companies, the CIA purchased sixteen B-26 light bombers, ten C-54s, and five C-46s and hired mechanics and pilots for maintenance and training. Shipping included two 100-ton ships, five 1500-ton ships, two LCIs, three LCUs and four LCVPs[1].

The original plan called for a daytime invasion southwest of Zapata Peninsula (the Bay of Pigs) in the Las Villas Province, near the town of Trinidad. The Escambray Mountains—the same mountain region in which my uncle Francisco had been fighting as a rebel during the Batista government—were nearby. They were chosen because the mountains had so much small game that you could practically live off the land for quite some time.

The CIA started to induct, in secrecy, Miami Cuban volunteers; the initial code name was known as Operation Pluto. The general plan was to build up a Cuban only force trained by the Americans to eventually invade Cuba; try to keep that a secret among the Cuban community in Miami. Eventually, a force of around fourteen hundred men was sent to Guatemala for training.[2]

While all this was going on, the Kennedy administration entered. We are all aware that, every time there is a new administration, for the sake of continuity, all information about everything affecting the nation is passed from one administration to the other. During this transition process, the new administration is informed of previous and current issues and any decision or pending decisions on current and past issues, so that informed decisions can be made. Of course different perceptions, viewpoints, politics, and policies come into play and affect the decision making of any new administration.

President Kennedy informed the CIA of his decision to change the original plans. About the time that I was on board the *Houston,* leaving the Havana Harbor, March 1961, a revision to the Cuban Operation suggested that the landing be done at night, with no concurrent air tactical support.

Out of the original planned sixteen B-26s, only two were allowed to bomb Castro's air force facilities. In total only six B-26s participated and just two or three of the C-46s were used. The final landing was in the Zapata Peninsula, southeast of the Escambray Mountains and not near these mountains, as originally contemplated. These changes would drastically affect the execution of the invasion, extracting a different outcome from the desired goals as planned by the Eisenhower administration. In my humble opinion, the changes the Kennedy administration made turned into it a plan to lose!

These plans were very detailed in nature. They covered political, regional, and national policies; military repercussions; cold war issues; and many others. Under the FOIA, released detailed, decLasified documents are available for anyone to read and research. I am not going to include here any of the details because this book is not a political dissertation. Many other books and documentaries delve into the political aspect of the invasion in detail.

In the aftermath of the Bay of Pigs, many Cuban Americans viewed the execution of the invasion as planned by the new administration as policy decision by the Kennedy government to rid itself of "noisy" and bothersome Cuban exiles.

This event convinced Cubans, by the thousands, that the Democratic Party policies did not have the political stomach to challenge the first Communist regime in Latin America and maybe something worse—the first Soviet base at the United States' doorstep. The fact that we were left to dry at the beaches of the Bay of Pigs had long-term electoral consequences resulting in the election of a number of Cuban Americans to the US Congress and the US Senate.

All I knew right now was that I was in New Orleans, and out of the clear blue sky, I was facing a life-or-death decision.

Chapter 13

Sailing for Nicaragua

I was able to observe the activities at the port several times during the two days we were there. Crates, boxes, and all sorts of equipment were loaded into the ship's hall. I was on deck while military personnel loaded drum after drum of airplane fuel. We were all admonished not to smoke anywhere near them. They drums were covered with wooden planks so that we were able to walk on top of them. Then came the speed boats; I can't recall the exact number, but I think there must have been about ten or fifteen, as well as all the bases for mounting the machine guns.

We completed our loading at the base in New Orleans; my ship was officially in a military operation. I do not recall our original captain's name. I have no clue where he went or what happened to him. Maybe his employer, the Garcia Line, reassigned him to another ship before the activities on board had started. I never saw him again.

The *Houston's* newly hired employees who had boarded with us in Havana and were suspected to be Castro's infiltrators were dealt with. I believe one of them followed my morning shift. I do not know exactly what happened to them, but I suspect that they were placed in another one of our ships and detained in Nicaragua. I believe we departed the military port in New Orleans about April 10; unknown to my uncle and me, his mother and my grandmother, Inez, had just died of a heart attack in Jatibonico. We were off!

I watched with a great deal of disappointment the New Orleans military port disappearing in the horizon. Although I never got off the ship, I really wished that this could have been the end of my journey—maybe a selfish thought. All of the original crew of the *Houston* had decided to stay and see this operation through. We talked a little about our mission; our consensus was that we would wait and see what happened.

My uncle and I had chance to talk about the operation. He reminded me again that our mission was to unload our cargo, as well as the invading force that we would board at Nicaragua, in the designated area. Once this mission was completed, we would just take off.

Our trip to Nicaragua was without any further incidents. I continued as usual with my duties in the machine room, but you could tell that a more somber attitude had befallen the SS *Houston* crew; we were not talking about having fun in New Orleans anymore.

We spent a couple of days at sea heading toward Nicaragua. The weather was nice. Thank God we did not encounter any bad weather; I think we would have been very busy securing and attending all the stuff sitting on our deck.

I believe it was April 12—I happened to have just finished my oiling tour in the ship's shaft—when I saw the entrance to Puerto Cabezas (Heads' Port.) Located on Nicaragua's Atlantic coast, the city of Puerto Cabezas dates back to 1690, when it was founded by English settlers. Nowhere near the larger population centers of Nicaragua, it was considered a very remote place and was a rare place for tourists to venture.

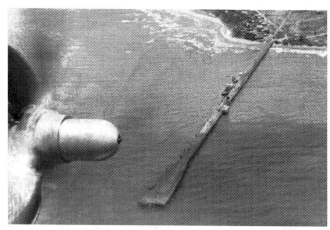

Puerto Cabezas, Nicaragua from the air. You can see the little village where we had our "National Guard" incident. (Courtesy of B.O.P. Veterans Association Brigade 2506.)

I stood on deck for a few minutes and watched. The view was strange to me. I guess I was expecting something more elaborate, like the entrance to Havana Harbor or New Orleans—the only two ports that I had seen so far in my "long" career as a merchant marine. I saw nothing but trees, jungle, and a few small hills along the entranceway; the harbor itself wasn't very large. And then we finally anchored.

My uncle related a bit of information about the operation. He said that three other ships from Garcia Line—the SS *Atlantic*, the SS *El Caribe*, and a sort of gunship named *Barbara J*, equipped with .50-caliber guns— would be participating. The SS *Rio Escondido* and the SS *Lake Charles* were designated to carry light tanks, trucks, and other equipment. The CIA had also contracted these ships for the operation. I could not see all the activity that went on out there during my shift, but I understood that we were loading more supplies; I think some of it was food.

The Barbara J the Houston escort ship.

The morning of the following day came, and I was still on board and watching at all the activity on deck. I surveyed the military men and the equipment. Some of the military men looked like Americans. I have not seen any Nicaraguan military personnel as of yet. The day went on, and finally we were given permission to go to ashore for the evening. We were instructed that this was also a military facility of the Nicaraguan government and that we were only allowed to be in designated places.

I took a shower and got dressed; my buddies told me that we were going "downtown" tonight. It seemed like a long time had passed since I had actually walked on land; I was so glad to get off that tin can.

The base did not look like much—a small village, huts, a mix of brick and wooden establishments. I guess that this was where the people who worked for the base lived. They all look like native Indians; someone told me that they called them "mosquitoes," but I do not know if that was the natives' real name. I did not expect much of this place. We decided to take a stroll first, to get familiar with the surroundings; we had no intention of going anywhere else.

I have this habit of looking at people's faces as they walked by. My eyes set on a very beautiful young woman. She had dark skin and a well-built, almost perfect, body. Her face was very pretty. Her dark eyes glistened and her long, black hair fell straight down her back. She was probably the prettiest girl in town.

Once we completed our stroll, the next thing we did was to hit the first bar we ran into—I think it was the only bar in town anyway—and order a beer. The name of the beer did not matter; I do not remember anyways.

I do not recall if we ate at this base or on the ship. I do no think that the cook would have wanted to cook that evening anyway, when there was real food available at the base. I had not been paid as of yet by Garcia Line, and to the best of my knowledge, no one else had either. Fortunately, for me, I had been saving a five-dollar bill[1] given to me by my father to use for a rainy day. I could not think of a better place to spend it than were I was right now, not knowing what the near future would bring. I paid for my first beer; I wound up with a bunch of money on my hands. I thought that was caused by the "dollar effect."

I was never a heavy drinker in comparison with my sailor companions. I think I had two beers, well, maybe three. Some of the sailors tried the local "juice." I have no clue what that was. The town around the port was very poor, far from what I was used to in a city. After our beers, we walked around some more to see what else we could do to entertain ourselves. We saw a movie theater, and a couple of us decided to go see a movie.

Inside the movie theater we found wooden benches. A cloud of cigarette smoke hung in front of the screen, and people were drinking and talking. I did not see any women, at least none who were decent-looking. The show for the evening was *Rio Bravo*, a 1959 movie featuring John

Wayne with Spanish subtitles. I had seen the movie before, since going to the movies was one of my favorite pastimes. Everybody was talking; nobody shut up and listened to the movie—what was I saying?! They did not understand English.

The moviegoers were very noisy and excited about this action movie. They screamed when John Wayne was beating up the bad guy, and when there was any passionate kissing, everybody made some kind of sexual remark or gesture, screaming at the same time. Lit cigarettes and beer bottles flew everywhere; the place was a total mayhem—it was great! I knew I never wanted to be there again.

The movie ended—I don't think anybody cared much—and there was not much to do in this village. Walking toward the bar again, I bumped into Lucio and Miguel. They told me that they had found out where the brothels were. I followed them toward a group of huts. How did they know? All the huts looked the same to me. I was really spoiled; I was used to the brothel section or "red light districts" that my friends and I frequented in Havana.

We entered a hut, or maybe a girl grabbed me and pulled me into the hut. I do not quite remember how it went. It was a little dark inside; with no electricity, the space was illuminated by several candles. The girls—there must to have been about three or four of them—appeared to be native Indians. They spoke very fast, and I had no clue what they were saying. But the stream of words sounded like a buzzing mosquito; maybe that was how they'd gotten their moniker. As the girls approached us to attract our attention, my better judgment was telling me, *You know these girls could be carrying all kinds of venereal diseases. This is not Havana anymore, and you have no condoms on you.*

I began to feel very apprehensive and uncomfortable about this whole idea. Some of my shipmates (they had consumed more beer than I had) appeared to be making their choices; apparently, they were going to go for it. A short, young, skinny girl approached me, took my hand, and invited me to seat next to her. I did. She took my other hand and stuck it inside her blouse on her breast. I said to myself, *I don't think I am going to go beyond this.* Okay, I moved my hands around her breasts and caressed her nipples. Wait! *What is this? Another nipple? No … I think they are lumps!* Now I was beginning to feel stupid for not knowing any better.

I was contemplating at this point running out of the hut very quickly and saving myself from getting sick. All of a sudden, I heard a commotion and screams outside the hut. I did not know from whence the noise had come; it could have been coming from a nearby hut. It sounded like a girl was being beaten up or maybe some kind of argument or fight had erupted. Whatever it was, someone shouted outside our hut that the National Nicaraguan Guard was coming. This was the first time I'd heard that there were Nicaraguan military personnel around. The situation must have very been serious if the military had decided to take action.

Not soon after the screaming started, I heard some shots being fired. Whether the shooter were shooting at someone or just shooting up in the air, I did not know. I took my hands off of the girl's breasts, and I left the hut in a hurry. *I am glad I still have my pants on*, I thought as I ran through the brush. Some of the sailors who were with me were also running toward the direction of the ship. The moon was high and bright. I could make out shapes. Fortunately, I did not stumble into roots or bump into a tree. I reached my ship in safety.

The following day, we were all going over the incidents of the previous night. Someone told me that I should have seen my uncle. He was dancing flamenco on tables. And I told him that they should have seen us, running out of a hut in the middle of the night with Nicaraguans guards after us, shooting in the air.

Do you remember that beautiful girl that I eyed walking about downtown? Well, guess what? Apparently, our youngest member of the crew, Osvaldo hooked up with this girl; I think everyone became envious of Osvaldo, our ship's waiter. A couple of days later, Osvaldo complained that he had contracted gonorrhea. The prettiest girl in town had left him with a "gift." Fortunately for him, the brigade's doctor took care of him.[2]

The following remaining nights at the Nicaraguan base, I behaved very well; I did not attempt to repeat the adventure of the previous evening. There was no way to replace New Orleans or Havana with this place.

The activity increased at Puerto Cabezas. The contraptions that had been soldered at the military base in New Orleans were actually base mounts for .50-caliber machine guns, one at the bow, port, starboard, and stern. I assumed that the other ships were being outfitted with the same hardware.

The reality of what I was witnessing and getting into—the unexpected chain of events, coupled with the mission that we had been given—was becoming more and more evident to me. At this point, all I could do was place myself in God's hands.

Chapter 14

Midnight Fireworks, No Fiesta

More military men in camouflage uniforms were arriving at a fast pace. I found out that these were the Cuban invading forces, the brigade.[1] I had completed my shift and had just had lunch and gone on deck. I saw an American officer[2]—I am almost sure that he was a sergeant—surrounded by several Cuban military personnel. They all stood behind the starboard, newly mounted .50-caliber machine gun, testing it by shooting at floating barrels several yards away that had been set up for that purpose. I was several feet away from this activity, so I could not hear what they were talking about; I guess they were talking strategy, the proper handling of the gun, last-minute training, or just plain target practice.

Several thoughts occurred to me. *The brigade has been trained for this purpose, but what if circumstances develop to a point that we, the sailors of this ship, have to join the fight to defend ourselves?*

Nah, I reassured myself. *We are just supposed to unload our cargo and the men during the night.*

But … we have not received any training at all, my brain shot back.

Hmm? May be I did not need to be trained, I concluded; after all, I was just an oilier on this ship. My responsibility was to lubricate the engine and its supporting equipment, nothing more. *Maybe it should be kept that way.*

My uncle Enrique told me, during our first shift, that we

would be sailing about seven o'clock that evening. It was April 13. Was there not such a thing as the thirteenth day being a bad omen?

It appeared that all the invading forces, supplies, and equipment had been loaded on board. The *Barbara J*[3] was our support gunship and was to be with us through most of our mission.

I was not to obtain any more details from my uncle. As first in command of the ship—not of the invading forces—he took direct orders from Captain Morse. I knew that he had to be privy to many of the details about the operation that I did not need to know. I understood this and realized that, whatever he did tell me, it was information he felt he could share with me, nothing more.

We started to get ready. The *Houston* crew was initiating its departure maneuvers; there was a lot of activity on deck and elsewhere. I had to hurry up and have breakfast. My shift was approaching; the SS *Houston*, and the *Barbara J* were the only ones left at Puerto Cabezas. Brigadiers were everywhere. The *Houston* was not a big ship, so they were all crammed together (I still had my cabin though). I fraternized with many of the brigadiers; at the end of my shift, my new shipmates told me that General Anastacio Somoza himself had come to wish them good luck at their departure from Puerto Cabezas.[4]

The brigadiers had a patch that read Brigada de Asalto 2506 (2506 Assault Brigade). I asked them what it meant.

One of the brigadiers in the group related the story to me. "One of our brothers in arms died during training. He was liked by everyone. We decided that we would name our brigade after his military serial number."

I believe, in retrospect, that the invasion provided the Castro regime with some validity of their propaganda at the time, which declared that the country could not go back to the conditions of the previous regime. Although there were some brigadiers who had been small players during the Batista dictatorship, the majority of the brigadiers were composed of individuals who believed in and supported the 1940 Cuban Constitution. The 1940 Cuban Constitution was modeled after the US Constitution, and was most likely, and in my humble opinion, the best constitution in Latin America. Castro's Communist regime replaced the constitution in the 1970s. What can you expect from a Communist constitution?

Thus far, our journey was without any incidents. During my free time, I made friends with some of the brigadiers. We talked about our families, where we lived, and what kind of work we did; made jokes and plans for after our victory; and shared our food.

I had a taste of the food that they had been given for the trip—boxes with canned goods, sugar, chocolate, and a few other sweets. They had to eat it cold. Most of the brigadiers did not like this food at all, or at least they'd had enough of it. I shared some of my hot food with them. One of the biggest complaints from the troops was the lack of facilities on board and the inability to cook hot food for so many brigadiers; our ship was never designed to be a troop carrier.

We played and sang old Cuban conga songs. You do not need many instruments to play Cuban music; an orange crate was enough to play some rhythms. Morale was very high. All of the brigadiers I talked to were describing what they thought would be their triumphant entrance into the country. They pictured themselves going back to their neighborhoods, seeing and talking with friends they'd left behind, recovering what had been taken away, most importantly, reestablishing freedom. The goal—to free Cuba and its people from a Communist system and oppression—was a worthy one.

The CIA had set up a clandestine radio broadcast operating on an island named Swan; thus, the radio station was given the name Radio Swan.[5] From this radio broadcast, we and the brigadiers received news about what was going on in Cuba. I was with my uncle when we heard the news that the bombardment to military targets had commenced. I prayed for my family's safety.

On April 15, two days before D-day, the *Houston* slowed down its speed. This bombing of Cuba's military airports and other facilities was supposed to cripple or destroy Castro's air force and its bases, and it was scheduled for today.[6] The Brigade's air support base was in Nicaragua, a good six-hour flight away from the designated landing areas for our air force support after the invasion commenced. This meant that it would take about twelve hours to reload and come back for support. I loved war movies—I thought I had seen them all—which did not make me an expert. The air force strategy did not look too good to me, but heck, what did I know about war strategy? I had just turned twenty-two.

We started moving again, but not too quickly. During my second shift, on the evening of April 16, I was informed that we were very close to our designated landing area; our mission was to unload everything we carried before dawn and get ourselves out of the area. My uncle came down to the engine room. He was to be in command in the engine room during all the maneuvers required for the landing. We all gathered by the air vent.

"Okay, listen up, we are very close to the Cuban littoral waters. Tonight we start the operation. Lucio, I want you as my backup. Desi, once we start, even if your shift is over, you cannot go back to your cabin. That goes for everyone who completes his shift at midnight, understood?"

"Yes, sir," we all responded.

"But we are just to disembark people and supplies and leave. What could go wrong?" I asked, and everybody nodded in agreement with my question.

"I don't know, but anything is possible once the shooting starts. From now on, we stay close to one another, okay," my uncle responded.

***

It was now a little past midnight on April 17. I was getting tired. My shift was over, and the ship did not appear to be moving much. My uncle and I were quietly sitting down by the cooling fans, deep in our thoughts, smoking our cigarettes and hoping that all would go according to plan.

It must have been somewhere around half past one in the morning when we began to hear heavy, loud shooting.

"It started," I remarked. I asked my uncle if I could go up on deck and watch. Our deck was very dangerous; we carried many high-octane fuel drums (about forty-five thousand gallons) that were covered with wooden planks so that we could walk on top and move around. I began to worry about all the containers, boxes, equipment, weapons, explosives, rockets, and who knows what else that had been loaded at the port of New Orleans and were now sitting in the ship's halls. We had the perfect conditions to be blown to smithereens.

Earlier, elite Cuban frogmen had landed on shore and marked the target areas. The view from deck was actually surrealistically beautiful. It was very dark; I could not see much in front of me, so I did not venture too far. The early morning was comfortably cool. After a while of conditioning my eyes to the darkness, I could see the faint silhouettes of the *Barbara J* and our own ship, as well as other ships shooting at targets toward the shore. The tracer bullets looked like red-hot dashes being drawn on the darkness around us. They seemed to move slowly toward their intended targets.

The tracers coming out of what I thought were .20-mm guns or higher caliber made the scene look like a fiesta, with fireworks and all. During this time, our ship's crew started to unload the eight speedboats that we had loaded in New Orleans; the outboard motors had been assembled in Puerto Cabezas. One curious point to me was that I believed the outboard motors were brand new, but I did not think they had been tested. The winches were very noisy as we unloaded the boats in total darkness, and the brigadier's commanders were concerned that they would be heard on shore. I went back to the engine room.

"I just got some good news! The brigade has taken Playa Larga (Long Beach)!" my uncle said.

"All right!" the crew exclaimed.

"My news is not too good; I heard up there that there were some casualties related to friendly fire." I had just come down from deck, where I'd been talking with some of brigadiers.

"Oh yeah, what did you hear? What happened?" my uncle asked me.

"*Barbara J* was responding to machine gun emplacements on shore. Looks like they were shooting back too low; they got one of our boats, don't know how many died. Other than the tracers, and faint light on shore, you can't see anything," I said.

"Listen, Sobrino, don't go up there too much. Just remember the two guys who accidentally shot themselves yesterday. It's not a safe place to be, okay?"

I just nodded in agreement.

"Okay, I'm going to do my rounds now," I said.

Our activity became more intense; the commanders needed to move our brigadiers onto shore as soon as possible. Our crews had completed the process of unloading the speedboats. Now we needed to get the hundreds of brigadiers out to the battle area as soon as possible. Darkness and the limitation that only eight boats gave us were to become worrying factors. I went back on deck again. Lots of activity was in progress; the shooting from our ship and that of our escort, the *Barbara J*, continued to protect the landing areas for our brigadiers. Someone said they were not moving out fast enough. I could only get bits and pieces of information.

Reports from the beachfront indicated that we had the advantage at this point and everything was going well. Those at Playa Larga seemed to be involved in the heaviest fighting. At this point, there was so much excitement and activity that sleeping was the last thing on my mind.

As the morning progressed, we started getting reports that the outboard motors were failing. A mistake had been made about one of the landing sites. The site signal was not pointing to the sandy areas of the beach but toward the sharp as a razor corals. In some areas, the coral was known as Diente de Perro (Dog's Teeth). Worse still, the sharp, protruding coral was damaging the boats' bottoms.

Time was running out fast, and we still had many brigadiers to disembark. The commanders and the brigadiers were getting restless and nervous. We, in the engine room, were also getting very concerned. We were aware that the closer we got to the morning light, the bigger the risk that we would be attacked by the Cuban Navy or, God forbid, any leftovers of Castro's air force.

Maybe our fiesta was coming to an end.

Chapter 15

Sitting Ducks

I looked at my watch; it was not yet 6:00 a.m. I went up on deck one more time, and I saw the faint light of the morning. We were still moving brigadiers off the ship. It seemed that we had lost some speedboats due to the conditions at the shore. I could hear heavy fighting coming from Playa Larga and also what sounded like heavy motorized equipment—tanks maybe?

I went back to the engine room; I had the feeling that we were going to be very busy. At this point, I thought, we must have completed our job of disembarking all the brigadiers, equipment, supplies, and whatever else. It was not a good thing that we had not completed this part of the mission before daybreak; the boat issues during the early hours had hampered our efforts to complete our task. Everything began to go wrong from that point on.

I took the steps down to the engine room. My uncle was smoking another cigarette. Lucio, Jose, Arnold, and Raimundo were all manning their posts, and we were all involved in our tasks. Our faces looked tired from the lack of sleep. We were not talking about it, but we were all thinking the same thing—we are still here; this is not a good sign.

I had decided not to go up on deck anymore. My uncle received an order from the captain to start circling the bay at a moderate speed. I believe it was now past six o'clock in the morning. As a precaution, I had lubricated the ship's axle and other equipment earlier than scheduled. I did not think that it was going to be safe for me to go into the shaft's tunnel as the morning progressed. *I will wait to lubricate the shaft until we are safe, maybe a few miles from the battle site,* I reminded myself.

All of a sudden, we heard very loud noises, as if someone was banging with a huge hammer on the ship.[1] Captain Morse started issuing evading maneuvers to the engine room. I could hear from the bridge, "We are under air attack! We are under air attack!"

The noise went away, but it came back a few minutes later. I knew that Batista had in his air force arsenal several Sea Fury fighter planes. Sea Furys were British-built turbo props and were as fast as the American P-51 Mustang. Batista had also had several World War II vintage B-26s, as well as a number of T-33 training type jets. It seemed to me that the bombings of the previous days had not destroyed all of Castro's air force. We were still circling the bay, trying to evade our attacker.

One of Castro's air force, Sea Fury, being loaded with bombs and rockets. (Courtesy of B.O.P. Veterans Association Brigade 2506.)

We were about a mile and half from the actual center of fighting at our port side. The attacker was a B-26 bomber. The *Barbara J* was close by and was directing her fire at the B-26. She was able to repel this attack.

We spoke too soon. Now, two B-26 bombers started their attack run. Brigadiers were franticly busy, operating each of the mounted .50-caliber antiaircraft machine guns in an attempt to shoot down the attackers. All the speedboats were now on the shore, and brigadiers still remained on our ship.

The same Cuban air force B-26 that had started bugging us made another pass at us, and then another airplane showed up for the fight—this time a T-33 jet. I did not see all this myself. I was still working in the engine room, and my uncle was busy following the captain's orders for evasive maneuvers. I was told much of what happened up to later by a few of the brigadiers on deck. One of our B-26s had tried to fight off the T-33 jet trainer; no match for the faster T-33, the B-26 had been shot down.[2]

The T33, trainer, converted to an attack jet, another of our attackers.
(Courtesy of B.O.P. Veterans Association Brigade 2506.)

The air attack seemed to have momentarily stopped. The second engineer, Jose, started to make his way up on deck. He was almost at the end of the ladder when another enemy airplane made another pass, shooting at our ship. Jose came back down just as quickly as he'd gone up. He was clutching his left side with his right hand. A bullet from the attacking airplane had made a flesh wound on his left torso. It looked like a big welt; fortunately for him, the wound, of about five or six inches long, was superficial. He was bleeding just a little, and he said that it burned a lot. We told him that, if he wanted to go up, he should wait for the airplane to complete its pass at us; I still do not know why he wanted to go up on deck. As far as I was concerned, I would leave the engine room when my uncle left.

"Full speed ahead!" Captain Morse ordered.

"Arnold, Raimundo, I need more steam, now!" my uncle ordered the boiler crew.

"Aye, Aye, sir!" they acknowledge.

"Full speed ahead," my uncle responded.

We started steaming away from the bay; soon after that, the captain issued a new order. We were to turn around because landing speedboats were going to be available to let off the rest of the troops. We made a U-turn and headed back toward the bay. I did not know this at the time, but at that very moment, we were pointing directly toward the shore. This little detail is one of the reasons I was able to write this account.

A few minutes later, a rocket hit us at our stern, but it only damaged the rudder. Of course, this was bad news for us. Now, we could not make any more turns. But it was just the first rocket. We got hit big time with a second one. I took a quick glance at my watch. It was about nine o'clock already. Within ten minutes or so, we heard another loud *bang* coming from behind the engine room (at least it sounded like it had come from there).

"We've been hit!" we all shouted at the same time.

I felt a heavy jolt. Water started coming in very fast, and I said to myself, *I think this is it!*

The water was rushing in very quickly; within what seemed seconds, it was already up to my knees. A rocket had entered through our flotation line, making a hole. Fortunately it was dud, and it did not explode. *Thank God!* We still had the damned forty-five thousand gallons of high-octane fuel sitting on deck, just covered with wooden planks! Up there too was a substantial amount of explosives, including C-3 and C-4, dynamite, and an assortment of rockets.

We were making water very fast. All of a sudden, Arnold and Raimundo, totally panic stricken, ran out of the boiler room. They rushed up the ladder leading onto the deck, shouting, "It's going to blow! It's going to blow!"

My uncle shouted, "Where are you guys going?"

Smoke and fire began to issue very quickly from behind the engine room, just before the door leading to the axle tunnel. My uncle and I were now by ourselves. We just looked at each other for a second, and he said, "I'll close the door. You get the hose; work to get the fire out!"

Everything seemed to be moving real fast. I grabbed the fire hose and opened the faucet wheel as much as I could. The water pressure (about 300 psi) from the hose blew me back against a column. I directed the water toward the source of the smoke. I wetted my T-shirt and wrapped it around my nose and mouth.

The smoke was getting thicker. I was told afterward that, at the same time, there was small fire on deck that was quickly put out, caused by an attack from one of the B-26s. The ship's crew and the brigadiers took care of it under the bullets of the B-26 and the Sea Fury. In the engine room, the water was now up above our knees. Fortunately, neither my uncle nor I had panicked, as of yet.

"Full speed ahead! Full speed ahead!" Captain Morse ordered.

"If I can't get us out of here now, we are going to sink very fast!" my uncle shouted.

"Hurry, drop the fire hose. Go to the boiler room and bring the pressure up as much as possible."

I had never operated the boilers. I had no clue what to do.

I looked at my uncle with my hands open and shouted, "How do I do that?"

"Pull the horizontal knob near the middle; pump it and pump it! Check the pressure gage; bring it up to the red marker. We need all the pressure we can muster! If we are going to die by drowning, we might as well die in an explosion!" my uncle shouted back.

I dropped the fire hose and ran as fast as I could with the water up to my knees toward the boiler room. Since the water was already so high, I could not see the floor, and I tripped over tubing from a pump. I got up just as quickly ad I'd fallen. I finally made it to the boiler room. I pulled the levers toward me several times, just the way my uncle had said. The firing noise and the heat from boiler were very intense. The strong smell of the fuel made me feel a little dizzy.

Soon, the boiler's pressure gauge needle had passed the red marker.

"I passed the red marker! I passed the red marker!" I shouted.

"Who cares? Keep going. We are running out of time!" my uncle shouted back.

I rushed to the second boiler and did the same thing, with the same result. When the other boiler's gauge needle hit the red mark, I shouted, "Done!"

I was still standing in the middle of the boiler room, looking up at the pressure gauges and waiting to see if my uncle had anything else to ask me before I left.

My uncle, following the captain's orders, moved the ship's lever to the "FAST" marker.

The *Houston* did an incredible jump in the air and sped up. Within a few minutes, I heard a loud noise coming from the bottom of the ship. We stopped just as fast as we had moved. We were already pointing toward shore before we were hit by the rockets; how convenient was that?

The Huston Burning, after beached.
(Courtesy of B.O.P. Veterans Association Brigade 2506.)

"What just happened?" I asked Enrique from the boiler room entrance.

"We just beached!" he said, coughing from the smoke.

"Shut down the boilers. Shut down the boilers," he called, pointing to the boiler room.

"Okay," I said.

As soon as I'd turned off the main switches, I came out of the boiler room.

"Let's get the hell out of here!" my uncle said.

"Well, I guess what we can scratch drowning, fire, or explosion off the how-are-we-going-to-die-today list," I murmur to myself, while cautiously going up the ladder toward the ship's deck.

For now, our maneuvers had saved our lives. We made our way out of the engine room by reaching the ladder and making our way, very carefully, up to the deck. Up deck was total mayhem. Castro's air force arsenal was taking turns on our ship, spreading bullets and death among us.

Brigadiers were running to and fro, in a moment of confusion. Our clothes were all wet from our little incident in the engine room,

"We are sinking, we are sinking!" the brigadiers shouted as they ran. "The boilers are going to blow up!"

Some brigadiers asked us if the boilers were indeed going to blow up. We reassured them that we had beached and that we were safe; as far as the boilers were concerned, we had shut them off. In reality, we would never know how close we may have come to the boilers blowing up.

Our support ship, the *Barbara J*, had just left us to face the enemy alone. The scene on deck was surreal; it was pure mayhem—bodies,[3] blood, bullets, and empty bullet casings were everywhere. We made our way to my uncle's cabin. About 75 percent of the *Houston* was protruding from the water, and a glossy oil slick was forming around the ship. During the rocket attack, while we were trying to save the ship, several brigadiers, young and old, had jumped overboard, in an attempt to reach the shore and escape from what they believed was the imminent explosion or sinking of the *Houston*. Many of them had drowned

The stern, where my cabin was, was under water. *I guess I can't pick up my personal stuff now*, I thought.

Another amazing thought occurred to me. *My God, I just can't believe it. You mean to say that all the bullets from the airplanes never hit any of these fuel barrels?*

I did not care about that anymore; we were now sitting ducks!

Chapter 16

A Shower and a Change of Clothes

"Your cabin is definitely better than mine; mine is under water," I commented in an attempt to make light of what was a very serious situation for our little adventure.

At first, you couldn't hear anything, and then a loud noised sounded as the airplane's machine guns hit the ship's iron sides. We both hit the deck, pressing our bodies against the floor as hard as we could. Another airplane went by, making a pass above us. The ship's metal cabin wall sounded like a jackhammer as the bullets hit. In fact, three airplanes were taking turns on us. My uncle and I got up from the floor as soon as the plane that had just attacked went by. We just looked at each other, as if to check if the other was okay, and then we had what I thought was one the strangest conversation ever, in spite of our dire circumstances.

"So ... what are we going to do now?" I asked my uncle.

"Well, let's see. First, I'm going to take a shower, and then I am going to put on a change of clean clothes," he said nonchalantly.

"You ... are going ... to take ... a shower now? What is that going to do?" I responded.

"Well, look, we don't know where we are going to end up, right? At least I'll be clean after all the sweating I did downstairs," he said, sounding very logical.

"You know that we are going to blow up anytime now, don't you?" I said, looking at him rather in disbelief.

"I promise you, I won't take any more than five minutes," he said.

"I don't think we have five minutes," I answered. "Hit the deck; here it comes again!" I shouted.

We hit the floor just as we had before. The airplane went by, discharging its machine gun fire on our ship; we had been spared one more time.

My uncle was true to his word. After five minutes, he emerged from the shower, wearing clean pants and a shirt. I was sitting on the floor against the corner wall. Our weird conversation continued:

"I can't even go and get my clothes. They are in my cabin, and I think they are wet. I lost my school graduation ring. My architecture text book is probably wet," I said it in a monotone voice.

"Okay, forget about all that stuff. Just follow my words. I have about four hundred dollars, which I am taking with me. We may need some money. And I think I am also going to take this little bottle of water purification pills," he said, putting the money and the pills in his pocket.

"Where are we going? We are not even out of this ship yet!" I responded. "And by the way" I added, "this is I meant by having a plan B. After pausing for a moment, I said again, "Whatever happened to plan B?"

"Okay, we just started plan B. Let's go and see the captain," my uncle said.

We hit the floor's cabin again, as another plane went by, and waited for our attackers to complete their pass at us. This was getting to be old news.

We practically had to walk on top of the wooden planks covering the airplane fuel, but we made it to Captain Morse's quarters. He was busily destroying documents; our passports had already been ripped up and thrown overboard when the first rocket had hit us. Other brigadiers were with him. One was trying to communicate with their headquarters, and I do not know if he finally did. My uncle informed the captain of the conditions in the engine room and that we were in no danger from the boilers exploding.

My uncle turned to me and said, "Desi, I want you to go down to the hall and report to me about the conditions there."

"Okay, where do meet afterward?" I asked him.

"I'll meet you on deck when you are done. Take your time. Just be careful, okay?" my uncle answered.

He remained with the captain, surely discussing other relevant issues.

This was my first trip to the ships' hall. As I was walking on deck, on top of the wooden planks covering the airplane's gasoline drums, it did not occur to me that, at any time, another of Castro's pilots would commence his attack and catch me on my way to the ship's hall. The smell of gunpowder permeated the air, and the floor was covered with spent cartridges of different calibers.

While making my way to the hall, I learned from a brigadier that a brigadier who had been given the charge of operating one of the antiaircraft machine guns emplacements at port side had been killed and that Julio, our quartermaster, in the heat of battle, had taken over for him and operated the machine gun. I do not know how or where he learned to shoot an antiaircraft .50-caliber machine gun. I do not think it was made official, but the word around was that we had shot down a Sea Fury and damaged others.

When I reached the hall of the ship, the port side door was open; this door was normally only opened when we were docked. Sunlight shone inside the hall, shedding light on the remaining brigadiers. They were quiet and just standing in place, clutching their weapons, unable to disembark. The remaining brigadiers numbered about ninety to a hundred. They huddled together, as if to protect each other; they looked very anxious, and some of them looked scared. *I do not blame them*, I thought. *I am scared myself.*

Their commanding officer was by the door with them. They already knew that many of the speedboats had been damaged, and none was to come back. They were also aware that our crews were lowering our lifeboats to help them get to shore. Neither they nor I felt too secure at this point, given the condition of our ship and the fact that we were surrounded with so many explosives and other dangerous materials. All we needed was another rocket in the right place, and we would all be playing our violins on the way up.

During the early morning hours, the trip for speedboats to and from the battle site was no picnic either. Many had died in the attacks of the B-26 bombers, the Sea Fury fighters, and the T-33 jets. Some brigadiers had drowned. I do not know how many speedboats had been lost, disabled, or damaged by bullets or the sharp coral reefs near the shore.

We seemed to have been a given another break from Castro's air force. Aboard the *Houston*, the activity increased, as all hurried to get these guys out of harm's way, onto our lifeboats and to the beach as quickly as possible.

I came back up from the ship's hall and walked toward the captain's quarters. As he'd said, my uncle met me on deck; I reported to him the conditions as I had found them at the ship's hall, telling him how anxious the brigadiers were to get ashore. "Tío, this is very dangerous," I concluded.

"Here is what we are going to do," Enrique explained. "We have the captain's orders to abandon ship, and we are going to use the ship's lifeboats to finish disembarking the remaining brigadiers. Our crew is already lowering the boats. We need to do this as quickly as possible, and we have to take the advantage now, while Castro's air force is probably reloading."

"Okay, what do you want me do?" I asked him.

"Stick around for a while; see if you can help them with the boats. We'll have to make a few trips to shore to get all of these guys out of here. I'll put you on the second to the last boat. Got it?" he said.

"Okay, I'll do it." I paused and looked at him. "But when are you going to abandon ship?" I asked.

"I'll be with the last group, with the captain. Wait for me at the shore. Stay safe, okay?" He put his hand on my shoulder.

"Yeah, you too," I responded, doing the same.

Chapter 17

We Have to Get out of Here

The first boat placed on water by the *Houston* crew was used for carrying the wounded; several panicked brigadiers rushed the boat to find a place for themselves. We continued to be at the mercy of Castro's air force, and at that very moment, another airplane appeared, flying very low. By this time, we had only two operational .50-caliber machine guns mounted at the bow section of the ship. With these the brigadiers immediately responded to the attack.

I was near my uncle's cabin; I ran toward it, got in, and threw myself on the floor, lying as flat as possible. During his pass at us, the Cuban pilot of the attacking plane must have seen that there were some brigadiers in their speedboats, as well as some of them swimming in an attempt to make it to shore. He decided to create his own shooting gallery. The screams of the fleeing brigadiers could be heard in the distance; all we could do was watch this scene, powerless. The attacker did this until he emptied his guns and had to go back to his base and reload. We continued with our disembarking of the few brigadiers left on board as quickly as possible; after the attack, we seemed to have been given another break from our enemy for the moment.

The shore was less than a mile away. I finally got on a boat. My uncle told the crew to watch out for me. I did not expect much, and at this point, I thought that it was every man for himself. A mix of brigadiers and *Houston* crew members were on board the lifeboat; we had to row to make it to the shore. I knew that my uncle would be in the next and last boat.

When we were about halfway to the shore, all of a sudden, someone shouted, "Look out. An airplane's coming at us!"

"Take cover! Take cover!" another brigadier shouted.

I was sitting at the bow of the boat. The only thing I could think of was to jump off the boat while holding on to the rope alongside the boat. *What am I doing? I don't know how to swim!* I said to myself. I took a deep breath and went under water, still holding on to the bow ropes. I could hear the noise of the airplane's engines and the rattling of its machine guns, and I could see the bullets splashing around me.

I stayed below the water as long as I could. When I could no longer hold my breath, I popped my head up and took up another breath. Some of the brigadiers who had jumped off as well were also getting back into the boat. Luckily, nobody had been hit. The crew was frantically rowing, trying to make it to the shore as quickly as possible before the next pass of the Sea Fury or T-33.

Finally, after what seemed to an eternity, I could see the sand coming up as we got closer to the shore. *I better get out of here before I get crushed between the bow of the boat and the shore,* I told myself. I did, as soon as my feet felt the hard sand.

The Houston after the fire, my cabin was the second port from the left. (Courtesy of B.O.P. Veterans Association Brigade 2506.)

We made it! I looked back. From the shore, I could see the *Houston*, smoldering, its fire still going and its bow protruding from the water. I moved quickly to seek shelter in a group of pine trees along the shore. Most of the brigadiers were there, regrouping and discussing how to make their way to the battle site.

At the shore, a brigadier was trying to make contact with command headquarters with his field radio; I do not know whether he was successful. Some of the brigadiers' uniforms were stained from the *Houston*'s oil. Others had lost part of their camouflage uniforms; some were without boots, and others were wearing only their underwear. *How did that happen?* I asked myself.

I sat down behind a pine tree, with the shore at my back, to rest a minute. I was wearing the same pair of gray Wrangler dungarees that I had bought at Sears Roebuck in Havana and a white T-shirt. I had lost my shoes when I jumped overboard. I got up to find a better spot. No sooner had I found a wider pine tree than another pass from the airplane started, directing its fire at all of the brigadiers gathering at the shore. We all scrambled to take cover. I believe that none of us was hit. I looked at my watch; it was around two o'clock in the afternoon of April 17.

I was beginning to worry about my uncle. I had not been able to see his boat or whether his group had made it to shore. I bumped into the *Houston*'s cook and asked him if he had seen Enrique.

"Yeah, he was a good man," he said, his tone almost monotonous.

"What does that mean?" I asked him frantically.

He did not say anything else. He just walked away. I thought the worse. I walked around a few more yards. I found a knife and took it, thinking it would come in handy.

A few yards away, I spotted my uncle sitting under a palm tree, eating a banana, a big 1911 model .45-caliber at his waist. He was with his second engineer, Jose, and Miguel, the helmsman.

"Uncle Enrique! I have been looking for you for quite a while now," I said, my voice filled with relief. "How are you guys doing?" I directed my question to Jose and Miguel.

"I'm fine," Miguel responded. He was not a big talker.

"Other than being sore on my side from my wound, I'm good," Jose responded.

"It took us a while to make it out of the ship; we have a few details to take care off," my uncle responded while finishing his banana.

"You don't happen to have anymore of those, do you?" I asked him.

"No, you are responsible for finding your own banana," he remarked.

"What are you going to do with that .45?" I asked him, pointing at the gun at his waist.

"I don't know. I found it on my way to the boat," he said, not too sure what he wanted to with it.

"Do you know how to use it?" I asked him.

My uncle did not respond right away. He seemed to be giving my question a lot of thought. And then he said, "You know what … I think I'm going to give it to a brigadier. After all, we are really civilians. We should not put ourselves in jeopardy. Do you guys agree?"

"Sounds good."

"Good idea," we all responded.

"Are you doing to do the Tarzan thing with that knife?" my uncle asked me, as if he wanted to get even with me for talking him out of the .45.

"Nah, I just thought that we may need it in this … jungle," I responded.

We had been left alone by Castro's air force for a while, so we were sitting around talking among us about what our next move should be. We heard some talk among the brigadiers of going back to the *Houston* to gather more supplies—K rations, water, munitions, and weapons— that were left behind during our fast exit, given the *Houston*'s imminent explosion.

At this point, the brigadiers had lost all communications with headquarters; the consensus among the brigadiers was to regroup and head off to the battle site. We could hear the battle raging at Playa Larga, a couple of miles from our landing site.

Whatever happened to our air support? I wondered. None had materialized. We and the brigadiers who were around began to realize that we had been left alone, on our own.[1]

Our little *Houston* crew had other plans in mind. My uncle asked us to have a little meeting and decide what our next step would be. We found a spot where we could talk without being disturbed. In assessing our current situation, we concluded that, since we had not been trained for battle, joining the brigadiers in their attempt to reach the next battle site would be suicidal. Our best bet was to try to make it out of the Zapata Swamps—the Zapata Swamps were south of the Matanzas Province and southeast of the Havana Province—find a little town, steal a boat, and head off for the Gulf and onto Mexico or the United States. We all agreed to follow that course of action.

I was the freshest guy out of school, and geography had been one of my strongest subjects during my years in grade school. I drew up a rough map of the Zapata Swamps on the sand, based on our point of landing. "You guys know that this map is not an exact replica of the Zapata Swamps but the best of my recollection, okay?" I said after I had wrought the map on the sand.

"Yeah, yeah, we know," they responded.

"I think we are around this inlet here. We will have to walk west, the longest part of the swamp. If fact, we are going to walk all around the peninsula, which will place us at the southern part of the Matanzas Province. If we are lucky, we can find one of the fishing towns and get our boat," I explained. "Do you guys agree?"

"Yeah, I think that is pretty close," Miguel responded.

"I agree," my uncle said.

Jose was not that familiar with Cuba's geography, so he abstained from making any comments.

"I don't recall the exact distance, but I think it's about 80 miles—about 150 kilometers—long to the west and about 30 miles to the northeast, maybe less. Okay, now we need to hear from the mathematicians. How long will it take us to reach our goal?" I placed the question to the group.

"I'll take it," my uncle said. "Okay, let's worry about the 80 miles first. Let's assume that we can walk about one and half miles per hour, depending on the terrain, and we may have about twelve to thirteen hours of daylight. At that rate, we could reach our first destination in about six, maybe eight, days. How does that sound?"

"Okay, sounds good," we all responded.

"I don't want to sound pessimistic, but that is, if we don't die of thirst and hunger, right?" I added.

"Well, let's not think about that now," Miguel said, adding, "Okay, so we reach our destination. Then what do we do?"

"We look for a boat, some supplies, and water, and then we cross the gulf toward Mexico or the United States," my uncle responded.

"I guess we need to be extra careful when we get there. They will be looking for us all this time, right?" said Jose.

"This is not going to be a short walk," I commented.

Turning to the first order of business,—we had not eaten anything since the previous evening—my uncle told us that the *Houston*'s lifeboats had a small supply of food and water, and we should go fetch them and have something to eat before we began our trek. We only found two water canteens, a couple of cans of condensed milk, and two cans of tuna fish. Miguel, our helmsman had a Swiss knife; it came in very handy to open up the cans. We all ate our share; come to think of it, this was my first meal of the entire day.

We started our walk. I believe by then it was about four o'clock in the afternoon. We all knew what to do and what our odds were. We did not talk much; we just concentrated on our walk. When the sun began to come down, we started to look for a comfortable place to rest and sleep. By nightfall we could not see anything in front of us. I think we had all run out of steam after such a stressful day. As far as I was concerned, I was exhausted.

The night was clear, the sky filled with stars, and the evening growing cool. I tried to go to sleep, but these damn little crabs started to bite my toes. To the east of us, the battle continued. We could see and hear the flashing light of explosions. We thanked God that we were still alive. Eventually, I fell asleep in spite of the crabs.

On Tuesday morning, April 18, at first daylight, we continued our trek, and the fighting was still going on.[2] During our walk west, we found coconuts on the ground. Given our meager tools, opening up the coconuts took some time. We shared the water and ate the meat. As we were eating our coconuts, we were startled by the presence of a couple of brigadiers. They had a sunken look on their faces; they were just walking in our direction.

"How are guys doing?" we asked them.

"We are being killed. I have no more bullets," responded one of the brigadiers.

They continued walking, zombie like. We finished our coconut brunch. Time when we weren't walking meant that it would take us longer to reach our goal.

After the bad news from the brigadiers, we became a bit more aware of the necessity of avoiding being spotted by Cuban patrol boats or Castro's air force. We took off our white T-shirts so that the sun would not reflect on them. That day, we continued on our journey without finding any more coconuts. The terrain was changing; more mangrove swamps were to our right.

I had found some abandoned army boots along the way; how they'd gotten there, I had no clue. I wore them for a little while, but they were too big for me. My ankles began to blister and bleed. I took them off.

Walking over huge mangrove swamps without shoes was not an easy task. At this point on the shore, there was no beach or sand; the thick, heavy roots of the mangrove swamps extended all the way into the seashore. Walking on top of the roots was very painful for me, and we had to slow down considerably. We walked over these roots for about two to three hours, until we finally stepped on sandy soil again.

***

Wednesday morning, April 19, was the beginning of our third day. The hot sun was making us very thirsty, and finding food was very difficult, almost impossible. We continued our walk, and as of that morning, we had not found drinking water or anything edible. I tried a few leaves of a bush called Uvas de Caleta (Caleta Grapes) to see if I could eat them. I do not know why they were called uvas; there was no sign of any fruit, and the leaves were bitter and hard to chew. After chewing for a while, I tried to swallow them, but I gagged and had to spit them out.

The beach at that point was much wider than what we'd encountered before. I started walking on the seashore to cool off; I was very tempted to drink the emerald-colored water. Since I couldn't drink it, at least I was getting a little cooling relief from the sun.

And then I saw them! "Look at that!" I called to the guys in front of me. "A couple of little crabs!"

Come to me, little ones. You are my meal! I said to myself. I was able to grab one.

"Hey guys, guess what? I got one!"

They turned their heads to me as I began to pull the little crab's legs apart and suck the meat from them.

"How can you eat them without cooking them?" asked our helmsman.

"Easily," I replied while sucking on a leg. "I'm hungry!"

Some time that afternoon, we encountered another small group of brigadiers that had apparently taken our same route. That day, our group increased by about four or five brigadiers. Just like us, they were seeking a way out of there. They seemed to be suffering from battle fatigue. We decided to take a break and sat down with them and talked for a while;

we wanted to learn about the latest developments. The brigadiers were a little loud, so we asked them to keep their voices down so as not to give away our position.

They informed us that all was lost. Their group had run out of munitions and left their positions; supply lines were totally cut off or destroyed. One of the invading ships *Rio Escondido* had still had a couple of Sherman tanks on board when Castro's airplanes had sunk her.[3]

After resting for just a little while, we continued our walk. We started to encounter small water inlets that required swimming in order to cross them. Between these little water crossing and the difficulty of walking on top of the thick mangrove swamps, we needed to rethink our daily mileage goal.

I was the only one who did not know how to swim, so my uncle and my other companions tied together some wood as a flotation device that would allow me to cross over; that was very nice.

As another beautiful sunset began, I wished I could enjoy it under different circumstances. The setting sun was our signal to start looking for a comfortable place to rest.

We have to find a way out of here. This was my constant thought.

Chapter 18

Getting Weaker

We were now on our fourth day, April 20; the sun was coming up once more, warming us from the coolness of the previous night, welcoming us to another beautiful morning, with the prospect of going without food or water. I noticed that, even as the youngest member of our little group, standing on my feet was getting a little harder; I began to worry about my uncle's condition, but I did not comment.

Ever since we'd started our walk, we had spread out. That way, we would be difficult to view from far away and less likely to become an easy target for Castro's helicopters, or whatever was looking for us. For the past couple of days, we had not talked much; each of us was lost in deep thought, contemplating the outcome of our efforts. I, for one, did not believe that we were keeping up with our own schedule, and not having food and enough water available was a worrying factor. I was aware that ten days without food is possible, but three days without water was dangerous.

So far, we had been walking for almost four hours, and we'd been trying to keep up our pace. It was now ten o'clock, and it is really getting hot. The sand was so bright and white that, when you look away from it or closed your eyes, all you could see were green and red blotches in front of your eyes. I wished I had sunglasses. And then a song popped in my mind:

On a day like today
We pass the time away
Writing love letters in the sand ...

For the longest time, Pat Boone's 1957 hit kept playing in my mind over and over. I thought it was somewhat weird, considering the circumstances we were in. I thought my brain was playing tricks on me, or maybe the repetition of the song was a way of putting a little distance between my mind and our predicament.

We'd crossed many saltwater inlets, getting wet and then drying up in the hot sun. Our clothing—at least my Wrangler jeans—was beginning to get stiff, and my jeans had ripped at the knees. I decided not to wear them anymore, as I wanted them to look as good as possible when we got to whatever town or village we may come to.

Actually we had decided not wear any clothing about two days prior because we'd gotten word that Castro's helicopters were looking for survivors along the coast.[1] We'd sort of camouflaged ourselves by walking on the sand with no clothing. This would make spotting us a much harder task for Castro's search party.

Sometime, about noon, on the same day, we'd encountered another group of brigadiers, maybe about four or five. We got dressed right away; we sure did not want to give the wrong impression.

We were now a group of nine or ten brigadiers and us. They had the same story to tell, fighting until running out of ammo. After salutations and briefly sharing our predicament, we again continued our way along the beach.

I still do not know even today, how it happened, but suddenly, about an hour after resuming our walk, someone shouted that he had found water. How? Where? I marveled.

We all rushed to where the shouting was coming from. Just a few yards away from the beach, in a grassy area with moderately sized bushes, several brigadiers were already digging up a small section, which appeared to be kind of muddy, where the ground was very moist. My group was given one of spots to work with.

With Miguel's switchblade and the knife I had found and kept, we dug up a hole about a foot and half wide and close to two feet deep. As we dug a dark, muddy, and smelly water filled up our hole. I could not keep myself from asking the brigadiers, "Hey, how did you guys know that there was water here? Was that part of your training?"

"Don't get too excited, kid. We still need to filter it before you can drink it, okay?" one of the brigadiers replied.

We gathered several of the empty bottles scattered along the shore. We took our T-shirts and placed them into the bottle's open neck, using them as sieves and, in essence, filtering the water. The water smelled like the mud. We did this several times, porting the water from one bottle to the other, in order to clean it as much as possible. We expended about an hour repeating this process. Eventually, the water began to turn light yellow instead of brown.

As you may remember, back when we were in his cabin on the *Houston* dodging bullets, my uncle had taken the precaution of bringing with him a bottle of water purification pills. Of course, this came very handy. We were so thirsty that I could not wait much longer to start drinking. My uncle put a pill in each one of our bottles, shook them, and told us to wait a couple of minutes until they dissolved and then drink. The water was cool; it tasted a little muddy, but at this point, who cared. I believe we stayed there for quite a while, sitting and just drinking the water.

I did not know what the brigadiers had discussed, but they had reached a consensus and decided to take off into the swamps; they left before we did. We filled our bottles one more time with the filtered water. We did not change our original plan; we got up and continued on our way.

Several yards away from the sandy beach where we had found so many bottles, we decided to look around. We found a bottle half full of vinegar. I thought that was very odd. I threw the bottle back where I'd found it. A few more yards away, my uncle was searching the sand. "Hey look! I think I found something good to eat," he remarked.

"What did you find?" we all asked in unison.

"A huge conch!" he responded.

"All right, now we can use that bottle of vinegar I found!" I remarked, walking back to where I had thrown the bottle. I picked it up. *I wonder how this vinegar got here to begin with*, I said to myself.

It took us a while to open up the conch. We gathered a few flat shells and put some vinegar in them, cut some conch meat, dipped the meat into the shell plate of vinegar, and ate.

"Come on, Miguel. This is really good. Just dip it in the vinegar," I urged.

"No, no way," Miguel responded. "I am not going to eat that. I don't think I can do it."

Miguel was so finicky. I did my best to encourage him to eat some of the conch and get some nourishment—Miguel had not eaten anything since the food from the lifeboat last Monday. I think that Miguel just did not like the menu.

"Suit yourself," I replied, making one last attempt, "but we do not know when we are going to find the next meal."

We did not find any more water or food after that. We looked forward to more of the same—more walking under the sun and sleeping during very cool nights, with nothing warm to wear. The nights were beautifully dark; I just looked up and saw tons of stars, without the disturbance of city lights.

As I walked, my mind wandered, going over the events of the last few days; oddly enough, it seemed as though the activities at the *Houston* had happened a long time ago. The engine room drama, the attack by Castro's air force, the burning ship—all these events kept running through my mind. I pondered, *How in the world were we supposed to have unloaded the fuel drums and gotten them to shore without the adequate vessels to transport them? Where were the trucks to transport them to our capture airfield?* I wondered how much longer we were going to be able to keep up to the challenge ahead of us.

I worried about my uncle's condition. He looked very tired. He was not walking as fast as we were, and I kept looking back at him. We had all lost much weight, and we knew that we were slowly dehydrating. We had finished up our water bottles, and the little amount of food that we'd had the previous day was not going to sustain us much longer.

We woke up on Friday, April 21, as always, on first light. Getting up and starting to walk was getting harder, but we managed to get going. It was already getting hot, and we were growing hungry and very thirsty. My uncle did not look any better than he had the day before; thirst and lack of nutrition was taking its toll on him the worst.

One of those time when I looked back to make sure he was not falling too far behind, I saw that he was peeing into his empty bottle. Then he dropped in a purification tablet and drank it.

"Uncle, what are you doing?" I exclaimed.

"I am sorry. I am very thirsty," he said.

"What does it taste like?" I asked.

"Horrible."

I guess it had to be really bad for him to drink his own urine. I was not at that point yet.

It was now the fifth day of our quest to get to a town. We could not see any signs that we were reaching anything that looked like civilization. We thought that we were about three days behind our original goal and still had a very long way to go.

A bit after midday, a nice breeze picked up, but the sun was at its hottest point, and the breeze offered no comfort. Once again, the white sand was blindly bright in front of us; we walked spread out as usual. Jose and Miguel were just a few yards in front of me, and my uncle was a few yards behind me. I wanted to be close to him, just in case. My uncle had considerably slowed his pace, so I continued to look behind me every now and then. One of those times, he was just sitting down on the sand, his head resting on his chest.

"Hold on, you guys, wait," I shouted to Jose and Miguel. "My uncle is down!"

They stopped and turned around slowly.

I walked back to the spot where my uncle was sitting down. "What happened?" I asked him.

"I can't go on any longer. Leave me here," he said. "Leave me alone and go away." His voice was noticeably weak.

"No, Señor Sanchez, we are not going to leave you here," Jose and Miguel said in unison. Jose and Miguel always addressed my uncle as Mr. Sanchez.

"I'm sorry. I just can't go on," my uncle repeated.

"I know we are all hungry, thirsty, and tired, but we must go on until we can't go on anymore," Miguel said. This had to be Miguel's longest sentence throughout the whole ordeal.

"Yeah, Señor Sanchez, get up. We must go on." said Jose.

"Come on, Uncle, get up," I coaxed. "Just think of your wife and children, your brother, your sisters, your sons, my parents, and my sisters. I'm sure they are all frantically looking for us. We can't tell them where we are; they probably think we're dead.

"We can't do this to them. We must try. We can't give up yet. We must try. You must try! Come on!" My voice grew more and more urgent as I attempted to motivate him to make the extra effort.

After about five or ten minutes, we helped him get up. We continued with our walk. However, for how long? It was anybody's guess.

There was no doubt about it; we were getting weaker.

Chapter 19

Among the Dead and the Doomed

Meanwhile, while we were growing weaker and running out strength on the beach in the Zapata Peninsula, our families back home were coping with the lack of news about our fate. Please allow me go back to April 17.

My family was aware that Cuba was being invaded by, according to Castro's media, sympathizers and elements of the deposed Batista government with the help of US imperialists. The media pointed out that these elements wanted to turn back the clock and erase the victories achieved by the glorious revolution, returning to Batista's time.

The following day, April 18, my uncle's wife, Aunt Mercedes, went to our home to tell my mother that one of the ship's invading forces was none other than the *Houston*. She did not know what had become of her husband, Enrique, and her nephew. My parents and sisters were freaking out. Of course, my family was already concerned with the bombing of military targets by the anti-Castro air force over the prior two days, April 15 and 16, and they were glad that I was not in Cuba anymore. Until then, they'd had no idea—no reason to believe—that my uncle and I were involved in the invasion, not to mention the extent to which we were involved in the Bay of Pigs fighting.

Castro's G-2 Rebel Army regulars and designated militia forces started a countrywide sweeping raid of the usual suspects—potential and known counterrevolutionary elements. Actually, this

141

activity had started on April 15, the day the bombing had started, and for obvious reasons, it intensified the day the invasion started.

The CDR was instrumental in identifying counterrevolutionaries. The search was systematic—neighborhood-by-neighborhood, building-by-building, and, for that matter, residence-by-residence, the forces looked for any citizen they suspected could potentially be a threat against the revolution. Of course, this included my uncle Kiko, the rebel.

Kiko was held prisoner for nine days, together with at least another 22,000 citizens, at the Sports Palace. Citizens who had expressed dislike of the revolution process and who the Castro regime did not considered loyal were held as potential enemies of the revolution.

The Sports Palace was not the only place where citizens were held. Another detention spot was the Blanquita Theater. It is estimated that over 60,000 citizens were held in various detention centers throughout the island until the invasion was brought under control.

After nine days, Fidel Castro personally came to the Sports Palace, and he finally ordered the release of those who did not have any known anti-revolutionary attitudes. The rest were sent to Cabana Fortress, across the bay next to the Morro Castle. The Cabana Fortress was a fort and a prison facility built during the Spanish colonial times; it became notorious because that was where El Che carried out the firing squads. I am aware of the Che's myth and the fascination around the world with this man. His face is featured on T-shirts, mugs, and posters. This man was a natural born killer; he just loved to kill.

Once released, my uncle went back to his job and collected some back pay. He was able to open up a barbershop; small service businesses were allowed in the first few years of the revolution, until private enterprising was totally abolished—where he made a living until 1963. Then, my mother and I were able to get him out of Cuba, together with his wife and nine children.

I would be remiss if I did not mention that some of my school friends, some who I knew personally and others who I eventually met, were actively working against Castro's Communist regime. My friend Orlando had a job in the administration office at the Havana Hilton, Orlando, was sentenced to twenty years. He was accused of involvement in a plot to poison Fidel when Fidel stayed at the Havana Hilton, renamed, oddly enough, Havana Libre (Free Havana). Free from what? I know that Orlando had nothing to do with the attempt, but just in case, he was condemned anyway.

Another friend and schoolmate, Agustin, was part of cell that consisted of about a hundred fifty members. The members of the group were taken prisoners during the invasion. Without the benefit of counsel, without a hearing, and without the presence of a judge, they were summarily judged by a "People's Tribunal" on the same day of their capture. They were given a variety of sentences. Some of the members got prison terms of twenty, ten, thirty years. Three were sent to the firing squad. My friend got sixteen years.

On April 18, the day after the invasion, the battle was still raging full force at the Bay of Pigs landing sites. The *Houston* was still smoldering from the previous day's battle with Castro's air force, and of course, we had started our escape from our landing site the previous day. My family had not received any confirmation that Enrique and I were, in fact, involved in the invasion.

The lack of any information increased the level of anxiety my parents and members of my immediate family were enduring. To make matters worse, other than pure propaganda from the Castro-controlled media, gathering any useful information was nearly impossible.

My mother and sisters became distraught after learning that my ship had been involved in the invasion; of course, they assumed that my uncle and I were likewise involved, but they had no way of knowing for sure. All they knew was that the *Houston* was our ship.

The situation became unbearable for my mother. On the second day after the invasion, April 19, news came that the *Houston* had been sunk and that its crew and members of the invading forces were either dead or captured.

My parents and my uncle's wife, Mercedes, visited several G-2 offices, hoping to get some kind of information, with no results. My mother did stop there. She went every day to the G-2 asking for information. Eventually, during one of the times that my father picked her up from the G-2 office, he admonished her to stop going every day, so as to keep her out of trouble with the government. Their efforts proved useless anyway. They just got the runaround. The absolute lack of results, of course, added to their desperation.

April 20 came and went without any news, other than the constant propaganda barrage from Castro's media machine. On April 21, apparently, the government finally allowed family members of the invading forces to identify their dead. My mother; Orlinda, Kiko's wife; her sister-in-law;

and my aunt Mercedes traveled to Playa Giron to view the bodies of the fallen brigadiers that were being kept there. Playa Giron (Giron Beach) was the town near the battle area, a town that the government was in the process of developing into a tourist spot.

My family undertook the gruesome task of looking through the bodies of 114 brigadiers. Searching the still bloodied and mangled corpses lined up one by one, they looked for us.

They headed back to Havana with mixed feelings of dismay, frustration, and a little hope that without finding us among the dead, we may be alive. This did not bring any comfort to my parents and sisters, as they now believed that we had been lost somewhere at sea or in the Zapata swamps and that we may never be found. Or maybe, by some miracle, we were still alive.

The captured brigadiers were televised and paraded through Havana City on their way to the detention center. My parents watched the TV avidly, searching for my uncle and me among the prisoners. During the trial of these men, the country watched as the most important individuals, according to the Castro regime, linked to the ousted Batista dictatorship one way or another, were summarily executed by firing squad, Che's favorite pastime. The "shameful defeat of the US imperialist invading forces by the glorious and heroic people's militia" was heralded and played out by the Castro propaganda machine to the hilt.

After all the efforts my family had made to finding us among the dead or the prisoners, they were in a total state of helplessness. My mother refused to eat and spent most her time crying. They had now exhausted all options available to them. Or had they?

My younger sister Zonia, only eight years old at the time, saw all the desperation around her and found this situation horrifying and difficult to understand. Her mother was crying all the time. In the back of her mind, she did not believe that I was dead; she knew that she had to do something, but what?

Zonia's answer to her questions came several days later; she remembered the Ouija board,[1] which until then, had been just an amusing toy to her. She got it in her mind that she could find out what had happened to Enrique and me through the Ouija. I had bought the Ouija board several years ago as a Christmas present to my sisters; we had not used it for some time because the Catholic Church had declared that it was evil and dangerous. We had put it away and just plain forgotten about it.

It was early evening; my mother was in her bedroom resting, and my sister Inez is also in her bedroom. Zonia retrieved the Ouija board from its tucked-away spot and took it out of the box. The board was a little dusty. She cleaned it up so that the planchette could easily slide on the surface. Normally two people participated in the operation of the board, but it could also be operated by one. Zonia decides that she would first try it by herself.

She placed the board on the dining room table. The radio played music softly in the background, not loud enough to break her concentration. She placed the fingertips of both her hands on each side of the planchette. After just a few seconds, and to her surprise, the planchette began to move wildly across the board.

"Is my brother dead?" She asked her question of the board.

About a half a minute went by. The planchette was moving rapidly across the smooth surface of the board, going around the surface with no specific destination. But then, to Zonia's amazement, it began to spell:

T ... H ... E ... Y ... A ... R ... E ... W ...A ... L ... K ... I ... N ... G ... A ... N ... D ... W ... A ... L ... K ... I ... N ...G.

"Inesita, Inesita, come here. Please hurry up," she called to her sister.

Inez jumped out of her bed and ran into the dining room, toward Zonia's insistent cry.

"What? What's happening? What's going on?" Inez said, not realizing at first what Zonia was doing.

"Look, I asked the Ouija board about our brother. See what it says." Zonia placed her fingertips again on the planchette. This time, it did not run around the board's surface but went directly to spelling the same message:

T ... H ... E ... Y ... A ... R ... E ... W ... A ... L ... K ... I ... N ... G ... A ... N ... D ... W ... A ... L ... K ... I ... N ...G.

Awakened by my sisters' commotion, my mother came out of her bedroom and found them looking excitedly at the Ouija board.

"Look, ma," said Zonia exactly. "I asked the board about my brother, and it said that he is ... *walking*. That means that he is still alive; you see, he is not dead."

My mother seemed a bit more animated. Still, she made no answer. They all just looked at each other in disbelief.

"I had a feeling all along," Zonia said. "I knew that he was alive ... but ... what does it mean?"

My mother and sisters seemed to have received a ray of hope for the moment. They tried to receive more information from the Ouija board, but nothing else came. They were left wondering how to react to the Ouija's message.

Apparently, my mother did not always share what was on her mind; for the most part, she kept my sisters from getting involved in her quest to find out what had happened to us. A couple of days after the Ouija board experience, my mother took Zonia with her and told Inez that she had to run some errands and wanted Zonia to keep her company.

She took the bus that would take her to Old Havana, more specifically to the Malecon Boulevard, and an area where there is a pier that taxis passengers back and forth across the bay to a small town named Regla.

When Inez and I were young children, my parents took us to the town of Regla very often. In Regla was a permanent fair, with rides for all ages—carrousels, flying airplanes, a Ferris wheel—and of course, delicious fair food. I am not sure if there was a way to get to the town of Regla by public land transportation; we always took the taxi boat.

The taxi boats were nice and well-maintained. I believe the boats were built in the 1930s. Some of them were double-decked and capable of transporting about thirty passengers. The boats were very stable.

We do not know to this day how my mother came across an address of a well-recommended psychic in, of all places, the town of Regla. I would learn later that Regla was home to the highest percentage of psychics in Cuba.

Regla was quite a contrasting town. The oldest part of the town was surrounded with modest homes along the main street, Marti Street. Beyond the main street were man-made stairs that looked down into a small valley known as Valle Oculto (Hidden Valley). In the valley were huts where the less privileged lived. In the newer part of the town, modern homes had been more recently built.

As for the psychic, I suspect that my mother's sister-in-law, Orlinda, had recommended her. Or maybe it was Mercedes, Enrique's wife. The psychic did not have any signs around her small house, off Marti Street; no one, outside her close friends and neighbors, knew what she was about.

Nor was it prudent for her to advertise her gift, given the attitude of the government toward religion and spirituality.

At the door my mother and Zonia found a woman dressed in a white blouse and a long skirt that had flairs alternating between white and light blue. She was wearing a modest, white turban. "Come in, Señora. Come sit here. You look hot and tired," the psychic said.

The inside of the psychic's home was very modest. There were some chairs and rocking chairs and a table with a radio. The dining room and kitchen were toward the back, and the back door was open to a patio adorned with a good variety of plants.

"Thank you. Oh yes, I had a long walk," my mother responded, fanning her face with one hand and holding Zonia's hand with the other.

"Would you like to freshen up with some water?"

"We'd appreciate that."

"Who is this cute little girl?" The psychic asked my mother, pointing to Zonia.

"Her name is Zonia, the youngest of my children," my mother answered.

"And how many children do you have?" the psychic asked.

"I have two girls and one boy," my mother answered.

"So tell me, my dear lady, where do you come from?" the psychic asked while my mother and Zonia drank some of the water.

"I come from where I live, Santo Suarez. And we had to walk here from the pier," my mother said.

"Oh my, that is a long walk. Tell me—I need to know—who sent you to see me?"

My mother told her who had sent her, and the psychic just reflected on this information for a few seconds. "Yes, yes," she eventually said, acknowledging the name my mother had given her. "I know her well. I'm glad she is your family. She is nice.

"And ... what is your name dear?"

"Martina Sanchez."

"I'm Maria Antonia. Tell me ... what seems to be causing you so much pain and anguish?"

My mother started sobbing again but managed to tell the psychic why she had come. "It's ... my ... son. He was a sailor in the ship that was sunk in the Bay of Pigs." She choked back her tears and managed to explain, falteringly, "I looked everywhere for his body ... among the prisoners. I ... can't find him. I don't know if ..."

147

"Come here. Come with me." Maria Antonio got up from her rocking chair, held my mother's hand, and led her, Zonia following, to a smaller room.

Along the wall, at eye level, were three images of Catholic saints, each on its own shelf with a small lit candle in front of each image. The images represented deities of African origins—the injured Saint Lazarous (Babalu Ayé), Saint Barbara (Changó), and the Virgin of Regla (Yemayá).

"Here, sit on these chairs," Maria Antonia said.

Maria Antonia went to a shelf along the wall where the saints were on display, took it with her, and sat on a rug on the floor in front of my mother and sister. She opened up the box and emptied the contents of the box onto the floor. There were fourteen to seventeen small seashells of different pastel hues—the number of shells related to the day a saint is celebrated and used by the psychic as her communicator; for example, Saint Lazarus is celebrated on the seventeenth of December, so seventeen seashells would be used for the session.

"I'm going to throw the shells for you," Maria Antonia said, picking up all the shells in her hands and holding them while placing the fingertips of her closed hands on her forehead and closing her eyes.

No more words were spoken; just silence.

Maria Antonia threw the shells in front of her. She studied them very intently for a few minutes and then closed her eyes and placed her hands at the tip of her knees. She began to move gently back and forth, and then she spoke very softly. "There are four men walking on a beach. Your son is a very slender man, and he is wearing a white T-shirt and gray pants; he is wearing no shoes. They have been walking for a several days. They are hungry and thirsty, but they are going to come out of this okay. I don't know when," Maria Antonia said after a few minutes.

Maria Antonia had described our predicament at that time to a T. How can the unexplainable be explained? Maria Antonia was not able to provide any more information. Neither my mother nor Zonia had ever mentioned anything to Maria Antonia about the message from the Ouija board. This reading and the experience a couple of days before with Zonia and the Ouija board breathed new hope into my mother and my family—hope that I was not dead.

Castro had been very successful in dividing the country. Cuban families and former friends were alienated by the revolution's ideology to such a degree that it was not unusual for family members or former friends to not think twice about turning you in to Castro's security machine if they discovered or even suspected that you did not share in or support Castro's brand of Communist ideology.

My mother's family consisted of four brothers and three sisters. Just to give an indication to what degree the rift among Cuban families had grown, a couple of days after my mother and Zonia had returned from their trip to the psychic, a knock came at the door. My mother opened the door, and two of her brothers stood in the doorway. They were armed, and they were looking for me. I do not know how, but they had learned that I had taken part in the invasion.

"Where is that son of a whore son of yours?" They did not even say hello to their sister and went directly to the reason they were there.

"What are you talking about? Why do you talk to me like that? I'm family. I'm your sister. You call me a whore. He is your nephew." My mother's brothers were very aggressive, and she was taken aback by their behavior.

"We come to bring that son of a whore to face the People's Tribunals," said one of her brothers, forcing his way in.

My mother looked them in the eye for a few seconds, and then she said, "Yeah, sure, I know where he is. Come with me. I'll take you to him." She took them to the bathroom, and she lifted the toilet cover. "There, you go in there. Go in and get him," my mother said pointing to the open toilet seat.

"Get out of my house," she shouted. "You two are a disgrace. I never want to see you ever again."

Although the spooky search for our bodies had not yielded any conclusive evidence as to whether we were dead or alive, the message provided by the Ouija board and the visit to the psychic had been enough to give my family some hope that we may just be alive after all.

Chapter 20

Ours or Theirs?

Saturday morning, April 22, we could not hear any more battle noises from Playa Larga. None of us looked very good. We started to discuss among ourselves the notion that we might need to surrender to Castro. *But surrender to whom?* I thought. *Nobody is around; this has to be the loneliest place on the planet.*

I pictured myself at a Revolutionary People's Tribunal, with the full knowledge that there would be only one sentence: To the wall!

When I died, it would be on my terms, not on their terms. I refused to be used as propaganda for Fidel.

We continued to deteriorate; I noticed that we could no longer walk at the same pace that we had maintained at the beginning of our walk five days ago. Miraculously and to my surprised, my uncle was still walking behind me. After the incident of the day before, I expected him to stop again at any time, so I made sure I stayed as close to him as possible.

Walking like we were provided a lot of idle thinking time; you constantly thought about how you were going to get out of this predicament. I began to contemplate the fact that we may not make our goal of finding a town or village from which to make our escape; one more day without food or water may just be it for us.

That Saturday morning, I had this feeling of peace. In the

back of my mind, I had resolved that we were going to die there, and there was nothing that we could do about it. I think God prepares you so that you are ready to meet him. I started to conceive a plan for my own demise. My plan was simple; when the time came that I could no longer walk a single step. I would find a nice, big, old palm tree. I would sit under it, watching the waves, taking in the breeze and die.

My negative thoughts were interrupted by Jose shouting. "Look, guys, what's going on out there?" Jose was ahead of us, and he pointed to the shore about a mile in front of us.

It was almost midday Saturday, maybe about 10:30 or 11:00 a.m. We all gathered to look at what Jose had pointed out.

From our observation point, we could see, about a mile away, a very fast boat making its way back to the gray silhouette of a warship. After what may have been about ten minutes or so, the same boat was speeding its way back to shore.

"Looks like a boat moving back and forth to the ship sitting at our left," Miguel said.

"It's a destroyer," my uncle said with certainty.

"I bet it's Castro's navy picking up prisoners. Don't count on me to surrender to those assholes," I remarked.

"Wait, not so fast. It doesn't look Cuban. Cuban Navy doesn't have that kind of ship. It's too big to be Cuban," my uncle said, animated by what appeared to be his second wind.

"I don't see any flags. Do you see any flags? It must be Russian," I said sounding very negative.

"Get out here!" my uncle said, pretty sure of himself. "I know my ships. I'm almost certain it's an America destroyer."

"If it's Cuban or Russian, you guys go. I'm going to the woods," I insisted with my negative attitude.

"Okay, let's take a vote. Those in favor of going to where the activity is and letting them know of our presence, raise you hand," my uncle said.

Jose, Miguel, and my uncle raised their hands. I did not.

"Okay, majority rule, let's go."

"I'm not going to turn myself in to those sons of bitches!" I said under my breath, but I walked with them anyway.

We walked toward the activity. As we got closer, about a quarter of a mile ahead from where we had seen the activity, we got dressed, meaning we put our pants on. We waved our arms above our heads with what was left of our white T-shirts at the distant ship.

Within minutes, the destroyer flashed its communications lights, in recognition of our signal. About five minutes later, yellow, one-prop recognizance plane—I would learn later that the plane was flying from the nearby aircraft carrier *Essex*—was coming from our west, flying high at one o'clock high. The plane flew by about twenty-five to thirty feet from the ground. We could see the pilot as he did his flyby. He waved his hand at us. I could even see him smile as he passed by, right over our heads. He then waved his aircraft wings in an up and down motion, acknowledging our presence. I could see the familiar and unmistakable American Air Force insignia.

We could not believe that we were saved! I could not believe it. Another five minutes went by, and a large, very fast boat was approaching the shore from the direction of the destroyer. The boat stopped several yards from the shore—my final punishment from Cuba; once our feet left the sand and got into the water, the rest of the way was paved with very sharp coral, like walking on razor blades. It took me several painful, agonizing minutes to reach the boat. My shoeless feet were in pain and bleeding, and I was the last one to reach the boat.

When we boarded, we found two very young men in uniform and two American sailors wearing their working blue uniforms. I was totally surprised when the two young men asked us how we were in Spanish.

"Hi, guys," said one of the American sailors.

"We have been looking for you. We were told that more of you were walking along the beach two days ago," said another one of the young men in Spanish.

"But ... you are Cuban, right?" I said to them.

"Yes, we are a special frogmen brigade unit, and we have been picking up survivors just like you along the beach since the day before yesterday," one of the young Cuban men responded.

"I'm very thirsty. Can I have a Coca-Cola?" I said as the navy boat took off. I did not even look behind me; I was so glad to be off that beach.

The powerful boat jumped over the waves, moving very rapidly toward the destroyer. The air felt good. The full impact of what had just happened to us had not reached our brains yet.

"No ... we don't have a Coca-Cola, but we have a canteen with water.

Here take some, just a little. Pass it around." One of the American sailors handed us a canteen.

"Easy guys, easy," the sailor exclaimed.

"Take it easy. We'll take care of you shortly," one of the young Cuban frogmen said.

We made our way up to the American Navy destroyer,[1] now I felt very weak. I guess I was loosing the strength that had kept me going for all of the past few days. Large groups of American sailors were standing all around us. They were looking at us quietly, with somber looks on their faces. I know we did not look too good. One of the ship's officers asked us to follow him. We were taken to sick bay immediately. I cannot speak for the others, but I felt like a ton of bricks had fallen over me. I felt that whatever energy I'd had left in me had simply abandoned me.

At sick bay, the doctor on duty thoroughly checked us out. He found us in good shape, in spite of our ordeal. He gave us a small glass of eggnog to drink and jump-start our slow recovery, and it was the most delicious thing I had ever tasted. About half an hour or so after the doctor concluded his tests, we were taken to a bunk area within the sick bay. They kept us there over night, to make sure that we were recovering properly.

I think we all passed out due from exhaustion—at least I did—as soon as we hit the bunk. I do remember waking up in a haze at some point to the sound of a battle alarm. The lights were red, and an intermittent horn was blowing, just like in the navy war movies. The sailors were very excited. "I hope they attack us! I hope they attack us!" I heard someone say. Apparently, the sailors thought that Castro was going to attack them, since they were operating in and near Cuban territorial waters.

Castro did not dare to attack. I fell asleep again. I do not know how long I slept. When I finally woke up, the sailors provided us with standard Navy working uniforms—our clothing was no longer wearable—and started feeding us with soup and bland foods to help us in our recovery.

I believe that about twenty-four hours later, we were transferred from sick bay to a bunk area with the general sailor population. About three days later, after we had recovered enough to be moved under our own steam, we were transferred ship to ship, to another destroyer—the USS *Eaton* DDE-510.

After making friends on the *Eaton*, I found out that the ship had played an important role during the invasion.

U.S.S. Eaton DDE510. (Courtesy of USS Eaton Reunion)
The Eaton was decommissioned in 1969, and then later towed away, and
sunk during target practice 90 miles off the coast of Norfolk, Va.

On the *Eaton*, just like on the USS *Conway* DD-507, we wore our US Navy working uniforms, so we just blended with the rest of the crew members, not that anybody was looking. We were free to roam on deck, to the mess hall, and to our bunking area. I was at my bunk when three young sailors came over to me. They all looked very young, about my age; maybe that was why they approached me. I cannot recall their names, so I will refer to them as Berg, Jimmy, and Peter.

"Hi, my name is Berg, and these guys are Jimmy and Peter," Berg said. They all extended their hands, a very friendly bunch.

I said, "Hi, guys, my name is Desi."

"You mean Desi, like Desilu, Desi Arnaz?" they all said in unison.

"Yeah," I responded.

"Tell us, what the fuck happened to you guys; we have been dying to find out ever since you guys were transferred to our ship?"

I told them my story—how I'd worked as a merchant marine on the *Houston* as one of the engine room oilers; I related to them my ordeal in the *Houston's* engine room during Castro's air force attacks and our ensuing long walk along the beach. They could not believe that I had been able to make it out of the ship alive. They listened very attentively.

"Man, that was fucking unbelievable," Berg said when I'd finished.

"We haven't seen that kind of fucking action yet," Jimmy said.

"Well, we almost did. You tell him," Peter said.

"Okay, several days ago, we were about a little over two thousands yards from the shore, watching all the action. We then saw a couple of Castro's tanks going toward the beach. They stopped, and one or two of them fired a couple of fucking rounds at us. One of the rounds went by the bridge; the other was too short," Berg recounted.

"So what happened?" I asked.

"Nothing," Jimmy and Peter said in unison.

"What do you mean nothing?" I asked.

"Not a fucking thing happened; I guess our captain either received orders not to shoot back or he was being very cautious," Peter said.

"But what would have happened if you'd been hit?" I asked.

"Fuck, I don't know. I think that if we had gotten hit, we would have returned fire," Jimmy said.

"We gotta make you look like a sailor. Wait here," said Berg as he walked toward what I presumed his bunking area.

"Don't pay too much fucking attention to him. He's just fucking cuckoo," said Jimmy, laughing as Berg walked away.

A few minutes later, he came back with a sailor's hat in his hands. "Here, you can keep this hat. I don't need it anymore. I have another one. Put it on."

I put the hat on.

"There now, you are one of us," said Berg, laughing.

"So where are you guys from?" I asked them.

"I'm from New York," Berg said.

"Jimmy and I are from Louisiana," Peter said.

"I was in New Orleans," I said.

"Yeah. How did you like New Orleans?" Jimmy said.

"I don't know. I couldn't get off my ship. I was in a military base, which was where we loaded our war supplies," I responded.

"Fuck, man, that sucks. You missed a fucking good time," Jimmy said.

"Don't tell me. I'm still mad about it," I said.

"What happened to your feet? They're all cut up," Jimmy asked.

"I lost my shoes jumping overboard the first day of the invasion," I explained. "I stepped on razor sharp coral, by the shore during my extraction from the beach."

"I got just the thing for you. I'll be right back." Jimmy went to his trunk and came back with a pair of nice-looking, comfortable slippers.

"You don't have to give those to me," I said.

"You need them more than I do. Please take them," Jimmy insisted.

"Thank you, guys," I said, moved by their gesture. I shook hands with them again.

"I have a question to ask you," I said.

"Yeah!" They all answered. "What is it?" Berg asked.

"As you can tell, I have an accent; is the English that I learned at school, okay?" I started.

"Okay, we noticed, so ... what is it?" Jimmy said.

"What is the meaning of that word—*fuck*?" I asked. "I hear you guys using it so often. It ... just seems that it's used for everything. I do not remember that word in my English grammar classes."

The three sailors looked at each other and burst out laughing.

"You tell him," Jimmy said, poking Berg on the shoulder.

"Nah, you tell him," Berg said, poking Peter.

I did not think of it at the time, but this whole scene looked like a skit from a comedy movie.

"Okay ... I'll try," Peter said. "That word is really a bad word; it has insulting connotations when used in an insulting manner, but we also use it when we are fooling around among friends. It's also used for describing copulation, or having sex. Look, it comes naturally. We don't even think about it. It just comes out; it's a cultural thing. It's hard to explain; that's the best I can do."

"Okay, we got to get the fuck back to our post," said Berg. "We'll see later Desilu."

They left laughing, talking, and pushing one another.

I was impressed with the American military; these young men, mostly my age, seemed to be ready and willing to fight to defend, not only their country, but also the idea of freedom.

I had read several books about American military campaigns during World War II, and I appreciated and admired the many acts of bravery and fearlessness of the American military. The American military troops had dealt with an awesome enemy; that was just something else.

The doctor gave us a clean bill of health. We felt stronger, and I got a very much-needed haircut. My uncle gave me a little money, so I was able to buy, as a memento, from the ship's PX Store a Zippo lighter with the ship's name and logo on it and a pack of Winston cigarettes. I still have that Zippo; the lighter still works after forty-five years, although I do not smoke anymore.

Another time on deck, I met another sailor—I will call him Robert. He was a little older and a little more mature than Berg, Jimmy, and Peter, not as much fun as those three guys. He said he was from Missouri, and just like me, he was a Catholic. I related to him my story, and then our conversation turned to life in his town. He told me about his family gatherings; I was impressed by the fact that we were not so different after all, that we wanted the same things out of life, even though we may have different paths to reach our goals. His plan after the navy was to get a job, get married, buy a house with a white picket fence, and have children. That sounded good to me; maybe someday I could work for the same goal.

After our first conversation on deck, I met Robert again the following day; he gave me his Navy Catholic missal. I still have that missal after all these years, I am no longer a Catholic, but the missal means a lot to me. I am not about to part from that missal anytime soon. I corresponded with Robert for a couple of years after he had fulfilled his service with the navy; I was then established in New Haven, Connecticut.

On the *Eaton*, we had several interviews with American intelligence officers; I assume they were with the CIA. A couple of days later, I learned that about twenty-six or twenty-eight survivors had been rescued along the beach at Zapata Swamps. During the dates of April 24 and 25, we were interview by the CIA intelligence officers. They asked us about the minutest details of our experience and what we had seen of Castro's forces, in terms of equipment and the like. Of course, my experience was confined to our efforts at the *Houston* and information that I had received from brigadiers along the beach before our rescue.

Another thing that impressed me about my stay on the *Conway* and the *Eaton* was the food; I believe to this day that navy food had to be the best in the world as far as the armed forces are concerned. We remained on the USS *Eaton* for over two weeks. I made many friends with the American sailors, but I spent most of my time with Berg, Jimmy, Peter, and Robert.

The attention that we all received from the American sailors was very overwhelming; their outpouring of concern for us was extraordinary. I will never forget it as long as I live.[2]

Eventually, we were all transferred to a troop carrier ship (again in the middle of the ocean). I will never forget the friends I made and the sailors standing on the *Eaton*'s deck, watching us being transferred from their ship to the troop transport. Unbelievably, they were sorry to see us leave, and so was I.

A destroyer, in comparison with other ships, is small; I sensed that sailors could become like members of a large family, even though we did not spend a long time together with them. I believe that I left them with the feeling that we had established a bond among ourselves, like a seaman's brotherhood of some sort, which transcended language and nationality.

The troop carrier was big in comparison to the destroyers. It even had a big PX store; a barbershop; and, I think, a movie theater. I was flabbergasted, and the food was great. I believe the troop carrier was bringing supplies and military personnel to Guantanamo. Unlike on the destroyer, I did not make any friends there; it was too big, and we were assigned a bunking area just for our group. I think we were on the troop carrier for about three to four days; our group did not disembark in Guantanamo.

We were all concerned that, so far, we had not been able to contact our families. They still did not know if we were dead or alive. I thought of my uncle's wife and his two boys. I could only guess that my parents and sisters were going bonkers trying to find out what had happened to me. Castro was not going to damage his prestige by broadcasting that a group of brigadiers had been plucked out of Cuba under his nose by the US Navy. Over a month and half had passed since we had been rescued from the Zapata Swamps.

One afternoon, possibly about May 23 or 24, we made port; we were told by an officer assigned to us that we had moored at a naval base— Norfolk, Virginia Naval Base, I think. Our group was ordered to remain on board the ship until later that evening when we would receive further instructions; our departure was being arranged. We were still wearing our working navy uniforms, and nobody could tell that we were a bunch of rescued Cuban invaders.

We waited until past midnight, when we were taken off the ship and into a couple of waiting, enclosed, unmarked trucks. They were air-conditioned inside. A naval officer accompanying us informed us that we were going to be flown to Florida and that they wanted to keep our presence under wraps. No one, other than ourselves, knew that the American Navy had been in Cuban waters picking up invaders.

We were taken to an air force base. I assumed we were still in Virginia;

the trip was no more than forty-five minutes from Norfolk. We boarded what seemed to be a paratrooper transport plane, four-engine prop. For snacks—it seemed to me that I was always eating something—we were given a box with very good fried chicken; French fries; and, of course, the ubiquitous Coca-Cola. It looked and tasted like Kentucky Fried Chicken. I did not think it was though. During the flight to Florida, we were told that we were heading to Homestead Air Force Base.

A little incident occurred during the flight, fortunately after we had completed our meal. One engine burned out. I did not have this on my how-I might-die List. The pilots promptly put out the fire. We continued with our flight to Florida with three running engines and made it to Homestead without further incident.

Allow me to fast forward for a moment to present day. For many years, I wondered about the whereabouts of the DDE-507 *Conway*, and the DDE-510 *Eaton*, so in 2010, I decided to Google them.

The DD-507 had been decommissioned in the '70s, as had the DDE-510. The *Eaton* was used as target practice, and it is resting somewhere at the bottom of the sea.

While doing the research, I found a nonprofit organization composed of former crew members of the *Eaton*. I contacted them through the Internet, and I related to them my connection with the ship. To my surprise, they received me with open arms. The group has a reunion every two years, and it so happened that they were having one in September 2010. I was invited as a guest speaker.

This event was very emotional for me. Even though few crew members who had been on duty during the Bay of Pigs Invasion were present, I had the opportunity to be introduced to several sailors who were on the *Eaton* at that time. I did not recognize all of them. For one, I had not been given liberty to be everywhere around the ship. Also, honestly, over fifty years had passed since that event. We had all physically changed very much. I had many very interesting conversations about what the sailors had witnessed during the invasion. Unfortunately, I cannot share the details of those conversations here, due to fact that these accounts may still be classified information.

I was even more surprised when the group awarded me an "Honorary Crew Member Certificate," signed by all the present crew members, as well as an official cap with the name and the ship's logo on the front of the cap. They had placed my name and the date of the Bay of Pigs Invasion on the back. Needless to say, I could hardly express my gratitude and emotion when the crew members of the *Eaton* bestowed upon me this honor. I truly thought it was an honor I did not deserve, since I was in the midst of sailors who had risked their lives during several wars and the memories of the many who had died doing so.

I am sure glad that the ship Enrique, Jose, Miguel, and I saw from the beach so many years ago was ours—meaning American

Delivering speech at the 2010 USS Eaton Reunion. I also received an honorary USS Eaton crew member Certificate.

Chapter 21

Hello, Miami; Good-Bye Alice

We landed at Homestead Air Force Base. The day was just beginning to dawn. Several tables had been set up, and INS officers attended them. A line was formed, and each of us was individually interviewed and processed by INS and given official US entry documents. At the end of this process, we had a final table to go to. At this table, we each received $250 and a change of clothing.

The *Houston* crew was informed by a Garcia Lines representative who was present that an insurance adjuster from the company would be contacting us to settle our salary and our personal losses during the battle. Many of the other men, not members of our crew, were already US residents and lived in Miami, so they would be going to their respective locales. We boarded several vans. My group (the *Houston* crew) was taken to a Howard Johnson Hotel in downtown Miami, and we had our stay paid, for three days, compliments of the CIA.

One of the first things we did while at the HOJO was to find the nearest Western Union office. I was still wearing my flaps. I wore them for about two more weeks before I could wear any shoes. Through Western Union, we let our families know our condition and whereabouts. I sent a telegram to my mother under a name that only my mother and father would know. I told them that I was fine and that I was sorry I had not been able to contact them sooner.

Over the following couple of days at HOJO, another group of CIA officers visited us to go over our experiences and gather more intelligence. I personally repeated what I had said during my first encounter with the intelligence officers and during my first interview at the USS *Eaton*. We expended some time perusing around downtown Miami; we just walked around town. I think we were still in shock that we had made it out of our little hell; I was. We needed a little down time to put ourselves together and figure out what our next step would be. Everything looked so new to us. The downtown area around Flagler Street reminded us of downtown Havana, where all the major stores and shopping centers were located. We walked to Bayfront Park to catch the breeze and talk about our future plans.

I would never forget the moment when I had my own personal epiphany; I know this may sound somewhat stupid to anyone else, but it was very special to me. On the morning of our second day in Miami; we were on our way to have breakfast. We came down to the hotel lobby, and I walked toward the street outside, there it was—a red 1960 Chevrolet convertible. She had stopped right by the hotel entrance, and the radio was playing:

Let's twist again
Like we did last summer ...

It hit me—*I'm home. I'm home.* You may say, what did you mean, *I'm home?* You were not born here; you had not even been to the United States before. Well, that is true, but since as early as 1954, I had gone to an American school, learned English, read American magazines and newspapers, and listened to American music only. My teachers were Americans, so I felt very American by 1961. Of course, since I was no longer able to listen to Radio Kramer and the Hit Parade in Cuba, I had not heard any American songs. Nor had I heard that song coming from the Chevrolet's radio before for that matter. I could not help myself but to ask the driver, "Who sings that song?"

"That's Chubby Checker, and that's a new dance called the twist," the driver responded.

Even today when I hear that song played on the radio, it takes me back to that moment in an instant. I never shared this experience with my little group; I did not think my uncle or my companions would understand my feelings.

After our time was up at the Howard Johnson Hotel, we had to look for another hotel, using the money we'd received upon our arrival. We found a hotel, Palms Hotel, that was compatible with our limited budget situated at 2nd Street and Miami Avenue. Today, the area is known as Government Center. The hotel is no longer there, and the area no longer looks the way it did back in 1961.

This hotel was where I met Alice. She was a beautiful girl.

Okay, I know I am going to be asked, what do you mean by beautiful? Alice was about five foot six—my height. She had shoulder-length, light blonde hair; deep blue eyes; a sort of round face, and a beautiful smile with perfect teeth. Her body was nicely proportioned—she had shapely legs, round hips, and a nice butt; she was just a little chubby, not the fat chubby.

She registered at the hotel about three days after we'd checked in. *I have to make friends with her,* I said to myself. *I like her.* Of course, I was suffering from hallucinations. What would a beautiful girl like her want with someone like me, a newly arrived, traumatized Cuban refugee, who had no clue what was going to happen to him later on that day? Nevertheless I fantasized. However, I believe that when something is planned for you, it will happen, and there is nothing anybody can do about it.

My chance finally came—I think it was a Friday. Our eyes had already met a couple of times the previous days. She was coming back to the hotel, and I was standing at the lobby.

"Hi, how are you?" I smiled.

She stopped and turned toward me. "Good ... how are you?" she said with a smile, but she also looked a little surprised.

"I have seen you a couple of times before. Are you also on vacation here in Miami?" I said, hoping that she would not say something negative and walk away.

"Oh no, I'm actually looking from a job here in Miami," she answered, to my surprise.

Okay, it seems that I am not being rejected as of yet.

I continued. "Oh you are. It seems that we have something in common. I'm not here on vacation either, but ... well ... waiting for a settlement from the company I worked for." I wasn't sure that I should have said it.

"Oh ... I noticed that ... you have an accent. Where are you from?" she asked, tilting her head.

"I'm from Cuba," I answered. *Is it that noticeable? I asked myself. Of course it is, you idiot.*

"Oh yeah ... listen," she hesitated. "I've got to get going ... but I wouldn't mind continuing this conversation ... Maybe tomorrow?" she said and started to make her way to the elevator.

"What's you name?" I asked her while she was walking away.

"Alice! What's yours?"

"Desi!" I shouted as the elevator door closed.

My uncle, Jose, and Miguel were all sitting in the hotel lobby, looking at me, almost in disbelief, as I had my conversation with Alice.

"What?" I opened my hands, looking at them. "What's wrong with making friends ... especially girls?"

"Nothing."

"I don't care."

"It's fine with me."

I could not wait for tomorrow.

***

I am having breakfast with my uncle, Jose, and Miguel.

"So ... where is your girlfriend?" Miguel asked.

"She is not my girlfriend," I responded.

"You know, you should be careful about getting too far with this girl. You sure don't want to get yourself into any trouble here, at this point in your circumstances. Do you know what I mean?" my uncle said.

"That's right." Miguel and Jose said this about the same time.

"I know, I know," I said. "But look, nothing happened yet. We were just talking. I don't think I'm her type anyway. It beats talking to you guys all day long; besides, she is much prettier than you guys. Don't worry about it."

We took our usual after breakfast walk. It was another beautiful day; it was starting to get warm though, and we heard that Florida's summers were brutal. We went back to the hotel, and the guys went up to their rooms. I stayed in the lobby, hoping to see Alice; we had not really set any time to meet. It was not until after 1:00 p.m. that she came down from her room.

"Good afternoon, Alice. How are you today?" I got up from my chair, or did I jump up from my chair? I put down the magazine I was reading.

"Hi, how are you? I'm sorry, what did you say your name was again?"

Uh-oh, I think I am in trouble; she does not remember my name.

"Desiderio," I said, sounding kind of meek. "You can call me Desi … I think it will be easier for you to call me Desi, instead of pronouncing such a long name … like … Desiderio." I couldn't believe I was rambling so much; I was sure I must sound like an idiot to her.

"Yeah … like Desi and Lucy … you know, the TV show." She looked at me smiling and nodding her head.

"That's it; you got it." We had gotten *I Love Lucy* show in Havana before Castro.

"So … what do you want to do?" she asked.

"I don't know. We could walk around a little. Have you had lunch yet?"

"No, I didn't even have breakfast yet!"

"Okay, let's go. We'll have lunch and talk. How's that?"

"That's swell," she answered.

I suggested walking to the nearby Walgreen's drug store on Flagler Street. They had a cafeteria upstairs, where you could eat good American food at very reasonable prices, and you could seat and talk all you wanted and nobody would bother you.

"So what do you think about the food here?" I started, making some conversation, once we were seated.

"This is pretty good. I like it," she said.

"So, Alice, what part of Florida do you come from?"

"I'm not from Florida. I'm from Georgia," she said, taking a sip from her drink.

"You are? I thought there was something different about you … besides being very pretty—like you talked … different than the Americans I've talked to so far; there's a little melody to the way you talk."

"They call that 'a southern drawl' in this part of the country," she explained.

"I see. I guess I have a lot to learn about America." I smiled "I hope you don't mind me asking you, but … you look very young." Notice that I did not say, How old you are?

"I'm already nineteen," she emphasized the word *nineteen* as if to tell me that she was old enough to be with me. "How old are you?" I think she wanted to get even with me.

"I'm twenty-two," I responded.

"I don't believe you. You don't look a day over seventeen," she said, shaking her head. "I'm from Missouri; show me!"

"I met a guy from Missouri in the navy," I responded.

"No. That's just a saying; its meaning is, prove it."

"Okay, here I'll show you my ID." I looked in my pocket for the parolee card given to me by the INS when I arrived in Miami. "Look at the birth date."

"Were you in jail?" she said, her eyes widening.

"No. What do you mean?"

"This word, *parolee*, all over the card," she said, pointing at the front of the card. "When you are on parole, it means that you went to jail and you have been pardoned or something."

"Oh no. Take a good look. See what it says about legal entry to the US. Take a look at my birth date while you're at it. See, I'm twenty-two."

"So what happened to you?" she asked.

I related to her a short version of my Bay of Pigs experience; what my uncle, my companions, and I had gone through as we'd made our escape without food or water; and then the rescue by the US Navy. She seemed to be listening to my words very intently.

"Wow, you are a very lucky guy; I think that an angel was looking out for you."

"Yeah ... I know. Would you like some coffee?"

"Okay."

I came back with the coffees. Alice's head was tilted toward the window; she was looking down on the street, and her eyes were somewhat lost in thought.

"What's the matter? I'm boring you already, am I?" I asked her.

"Oh, no ... no ... I was just thinking," she responded while opening her sugar packet.

"Is there anything that you would want to share with me, or is that too personal a question?"

"Well ... I hope that you don't get the wrong impression about me, but I'm actually running away," she said softly.

"Running away? From what?"

"It's like this. I got married about six months ago—"

"Isn't that kind of young?" I interrupted.

"Yeah ... I know, I agree." She paused, as if in thought. "Anyway, everything looked fine in the beginning between my husband and me, and then out of nowhere, he began to ... physically abuse me." She sighed. "At first I thought that it was just a brief thing that couples go through at the beginning of their relationship, but when it didn't stop ... I left." Her voice drifted off. "I didn't know what else to do," she continued.

"Were you afraid of him? Did you tell your parents where you were going?"

"Yes I was ... I am. No, I haven't called my parents yet."

"Don't you think they are worried about you? You have to call them and let them know."

I left it at that I did not want to inquire anymore.

We walked back to the hotel, and we talked about our efforts at finding a job and how she was going to be busy starting Monday with some interviews. I did not have any interviews coming up yet.

"Do you mind if I walk up with you to your room?" I asked.

"No, come on." We stepped into the elevator and started our way up slowly.

We stopped by her room door, and I held her hand. "Alice, I really had a good time with you today. I hope you did too. Maybe I'll see you sometime tomorrow, okay?" I just started to walk away.

"Wait. Desi ... wait. Do you mind coming in for just a little while?" She looked at me with a look that only a woman can give, and you just have to say, *yes*!

"Okay," I responded.

I do not know how it happened, but before I knew it, we were twisting and turning, making passionate love. I think we both needed that human touch. I know I needed it badly, and I think she did too. And of course the experience was much better because we had taken a liking to each other.

I did not see Alice for a couple of days after our Walgreen's lunch and our sexual encounter, but I knew she was busy looking for a job.

Miami was a nice place to spend a vacation. My grandparents on my father's side came every year to vacation at Miami Beach. But in 1961, finding work was not easy. The month of June was now starting, and the summer season was approaching. Winter in the north was over, and businesses in Miami would experience a decline in business, and along with it jobs openings, all throughout the summer.

Enrique got a job at a Sugar Mill in Pahokee maintaining the mill's electrical equipment. In Cuba, besides his job as a chief engineer at Garcia Line, he had operated a small business, rebuilding electric motors.

Alice got a job with Southern Bell—today known as BellSouth. Alice introduced me to her new boyfriend, who she'd met at work. She told me that, by the following week, she was going to live in her own apartment. I told her that I was really happy that all had worked out for her.

Although I really did not hold any ill feelings toward Alice, I could not help but feel a little rejected. There was nothing really serious between her and me, and I had not expected our sexual encounter to become meaningful or go anywhere, especially given my circumstances. Still, a song that I had recently heard by Dion came to mind:

Here's my story, it's sad but true
It's about a girl that I once knew ...

It just made me feel better.

Within a week, Alice moved out of the Palms Hotel. I never saw her again.

Chapter 22

Connecticut or Bust

By mid-June 1961, I was still trying to find work in Miami, particularly in the accounting area, since that was my major at college. I bought a couple of sport jackets, dress shirts, and ties at Burdines—a premier department store in South Florida for many years (recently bought out by Macy's) so that I would be ready for any job interview that may come along. I had contacted a couple of employment agents and filled out applications, but nothing had panned out for the moment.

I was running out of my insurance money. I contacted the Knights of Columbus in New Haven, Connecticut, by writing a letter to Mr. William Piedmont, Columbian Squires Division. I related to him my harrowing experience at the Bay of Pigs and my current predicament. Mr. Piedmont, in turn, contacted a Columbian Squire leader working with a Father Fox and involved with the Cuban refugee's plight in Duluth, Minnesota. I didn't know anybody in Duluth, Minnesota. Was that not that place that got very cold in the winter?

No way. Instead, I decided to buy a one-way ticket to New Haven, Connecticut, and take my chances there.

I sent a letter to my friend Emilio, Rodi's brother, in New Haven. I explained to him my predicament, and I asked him if he would mind taking me in for about a month, until I got on my feet. He said that he would help me out. I bought a one-way Greyhound bus ticket. It was Connecticut or bust!

I was very excited about my trip to Connecticut. I knew that Connecticut was rich in American history; also New Haven was famous for being the home of Yale University as well as for playing key roles during the inception of the American Constitution, as one of the original thirteen colonies. I saw many towns along the way, as well as beautiful landscape, through the window of my Greyhound bus. The bus took about two days to get to New Haven. I loved that town.

The day of my arrival in New Haven, and to the amazement of Mr. Piedmont, I showed up to apply for a job at the Knights of Columbus headquarters. Mr. Piedmont was in charge of the Columbian Squires, nationally and internationally. I told him that I felt very uncomfortable going to where he had suggested, Duluth, Minnesota, because I knew no one there but that I had a friend from home already living in New Haven. He told me, to my surprise, that there was a Cuban already working at the Knights of Columbus, Mr. Jorge Hyatt. I knew Mr. Hyatt; he had an important position at the Knights of Columbus and had held a high office in the K of C organization in Havana. Mr. Piedmont took me to meet him at his office.

Mr. Hyatt and I shook hands, and he said to me, "I remember you!"

I related to him my experience during the invasion. He listened to my story attentively, commenting that he could not believe I had made it out alive.

Mr. Piedmont took me to the personnel department and had me fill out a job application. The personnel department (now human resources) director told me to come back the following Monday.

I was at the K of C headquarters building early that Monday morning; I needed this job. I was already thinking of my next challenge, which was to bring my mother and sisters to the United States and spare them from the hell that awaited them in Cuba. The K of C personnel manager informed me that the headquarters had a summer program for college students and that two of the students would be leaving in a couple of weeks to go back to college. From my job application, he knew that I had graduated in accounting, but they did not have any openings in that department at this point. There was, however, a job opening was in the computer department; I would bring supplies to the IBM machine operators. And eventually, I would have a chance to learn the IBM machines. At this point, my choices were very limited; I took the job.

I was in awe when I learned that my coworkers were from so many parts of the world. People from Ukraine, Poland, Germany, France, Italy, England, Mexico, Ireland, Hungary, and many other countries were all working together—a microcosm of what the world could be if you were an American.

Somehow, I managed to have fun, in the midst of absorbing the culture and establishing myself in the citizenry. I felt very welcome from the very first day of work at K of C. Fred Palcovich and Jimmy Heffernan extended their friendship to me. Fred was about five foot six; had short, dark blond hair; and was a little chubby. He resembled Lawrence Welk. Although he would never tell anyone his age, everyone suspected that he was in his early forties when I met him. Fred ended almost every sentence with "in other words."

Jimmy was about five foot eight. He was beginning to lose his short-cropped, dark hair. Jimmy was in his early thirties when I met him. His English was a little difficult to understand; it was not him, it was me with the problem. I had to train my ear on him to make sure I understood what he was saying. He did not have speech impediment; he just spoke differently. Jimmy introduced me to all of his friend at Cassidy's, an Irish Pub where I became a frequent visitor and made another group of friends.

However, it was Fred who took me under his wing and took me everywhere. One of my first social experiences was in the home of one of Fred's friends, at a celebrate Friday party. Among the guests were people from the office and others. Fred's friend was an Irishman—I cannot recall his name, but I learned later that he had something to do with a union. Fred made sure that I felt comfortable with everyone, and he introduced me to all who were present.

During the course of the party, Fred kept my scotch and soda glass always fresh, to the point that I passed out while I was in the kitchen preparing myself another drink. I vaguely remember waking up sometime during the evening, lying on the front lawn of Fred's friend house. I remember thinking, *What happened? Why is the moon so close to my eyes?* It was not the moon; it was the light on the lamppost. I was incapacitated for the rest of the weekend; I thought I was going to die. I barely made it to work the following Monday.

Fred loved ice hockey, and the New Haven Blades. New York's Johnstown Jets and Long Island Ducks were our rivals. Of course, we rooted for the home team. New Haven was now my home. I was not going back to Cuba anytime soon. Fred always made sure that I went with him to the games; he would pick me up in his brand-new Dodge Dart. Fred traded in his car every year.

I had never been a sports fan, but I actually enjoyed the game of ice hockey. After the hockey game, the cool thing to do was to go to West Haven's Saving Rock.

Saving Rock was a beach area west of New Haven overlooking the New Haven Harbor and the Long Island Sound. In West Haven, during the summer months, dragsters had Saturday night car races. A huge rock—guess where the beach got its name—about two stories high and close to a hundred feet long, was located near an indoor/outdoor restaurant named Jimmy's at the Rock. Besides Jimmy's, there were other restaurants around, such as Phyllis's, which catered to an older crowed. But Jimmy's was the place to be. Inside the restaurant, where Fred and I always invariably went, we always ordered the same thing—a pile high of New England fried clams and French fries. I could not help myself; the meal was fantastic. Everything that I was experiencing was so new to me.

Fred and I would talk about the game and work, and then he would often talk about the love of his life, Rosemary Cooney. Fred was crazy about Rosemary, but he never dared to talk to her about it. I guess that rejection is man's worse enemy. Personally, I was of the opinion that Rosemary was just a dream for Fred, just like Emelia had been a dream for me. I thought that he did not have a chance with Rosemary. I think deep inside he knew it too.

Outside, in Jimmy's parking lot, lots of young men were "cruising" around looking for "chicks," practically all night. Parked in the lot were souped-up hot rods, just like in the movies, 1957 Thunderbirds, 1961 Chevy SS Impalas, 1956 Ford Victorias, 1961 Bonneville convertibles, and many others. Music blasted from the car's radios, playing songs like Bobby Lewis's "Tossing and Turning," Del Shannon's "Runaway," Bobby Vee's "Take Good Care of My Baby," and Ray Charles's "Hit the Road, Jack." Jimmy's was famous for the hot dogs, hamburgers, and French fries just flying out their outdoor counters. I loved it; I'd found a true "American Graffiti." Fred and I spent many good times together. Unfortunately, he died in the early 1970s of a massive heart attack. I really missed the guy.

I started collecting a weekly salary, and within a month, I left Emilio's home. I had gathered enough money to rent my first apartment. I found a nice little apartment in downtown New Haven, with the help of Mr. Hyatt's son George Jr. Mr. Hyatt had left Havana with his wife and their only son George Jr. in 1960. George Jr. was about my height. He had slightly curly hair, lighter skin than mine, and a very pleasant face. Although he was about my age, he looked a lot older than me. Not as reserved as I was, he was always smiling. He knew all the ropes around New Haven—a good connection, I thought.

The apartment was located on 84 Wall Street, a very desirable location right smack in the middle of Yale University campus. Young men would kill just to live there. My apartment was on the second floor above a barbershop and next to a pizza place frequented by students.

I was really surprised a year later when one of the employees from the pizza parlor came up looking for me at my apartment to tell me that my mother had phoned me to let me know about their arrival in Miami.

Come to think of it, George had ulterior motives for helping me find a place of my own. He got to use the apartment also, during our many encounters with females. I did not mind at the time; I was alone anyway. The apartment was in a great

My first apartment in New Haven, Conn. July 1961, at the corner is the same Pizza place, at 90 Wall St. My apartment was on the second floor 84 Wall St. To the left is one of the many colleges at Yale University. Circa 2008.

location, two blocks from the New Haven Green and less than four blocks from work. New Haven was just beautiful during spring, summer, and fall. It was brutal during the New England winter. I had no car, so I walked back and forth between work and home.

Because of George's uncanny ability to attract the opposite sex, I was not alone for too long. George met Roberta and Joyce. Roberta was from Russia. She had light brown hair, was about five foot five and slender, and had a nicely shaped body and a nice, friendly personality. Joyce was from an Italian family. She had black, wavy hair, white skin, and a sort of Roman nose. She was heavy boned but not fat and reserved but friendly. Roberta and Joyce were nursing residents at Yale New Haven Hospital.

Sometimes, George was alone with Roberta in my apartment, so I went to the movies. Other times, based on their scheduled, I was alone with Joyce and George was at the movies. Other times, we were all at my apartment. Or occasionally, we went to Joyce and Roberta's dorm; of course we had to sneak in. George eventually married Roberta, and he was still married to her when I talked to him back in the late 1980s.

Joyce and I got along very well. We never argued and had interesting conversations. We had a good time together, considering our limited budget; she was a student, and I was a struggling Cuban refugee. Joyce came from a very strict, old-fashioned Italian family. She and I went out together for almost a year. We always made out like crazy, but we never had a sexual relationship—not that I didn't try. But all I had to hear was *no* once, and I would not try again. I did not like to be embarrassed twice.

Joyce was saving herself for a very special person. I knew that she was because one day I received a very nice letter from her.

She wrote in the letter that she was falling in love with me but that I would not qualify with her family, based on my status as a Cuban refugee and not a US citizen, and that I may not be in a position to offer her the safety and stability that most women want from her man. She went on, explaining that rather than causing heartache for her and her family, it was best that we not see each other again. I thought that was a very smart and civilized way to dump me. Actually, I agreed with her assessment of our relationship. I was a newcomer; I had many things I needed to focus on—my family's attempt flee Cuba and, of course, my future not least among them. I still had to wait about five years before I could apply for US citizenship.

The remainder of 1961 and the first few months of 1962 were very busy for me. I was very comfortable with my new surroundings. It did not take me long to be promoted to the operations of the IBM machines. Meanwhile, I was busy making contacts to bring my family out of Cuba to the United States. After receiving much help from friends and coworkers at the K of C and from Connecticut's then Senator Prescott Bush (father of President George H. Bush), I was able to get my mother and sisters—my father had remarried and did not wanted to leave—out of Cuba just a few months before the October Cuban Missile Crisis.

Back in Cuba, the government had implemented a food rationing system—"Control De Ventas Para Productos Alimenticios" (Control for Purchasing Food Products). The groceries stores that had once been full of food supplies under the evil capitalist system were rapidly being depleted. Many of the food products were coming from the Soviet Union and Soviet Bloc countries. My mother got really sick from a can of bear meat imported from the former Soviet Union.

The control booklet covered fuel for cooking, meat, poultry, and vegetables. It included a page for each month of the year and only sixteen items per page. A page listed the kinds of fuel the family utilized for cooking—electricity, gas, kerosene, liquid gas—and even whether or not you had a pressure cooker.

Another monthly set of pages controlled specific products, including meat products and milk products, and finally, another set of monthly pages was for bread only. The names of each of the family members who were allowed to purchase the products were also listed in the booklet. Families were assigned a store number; you could only buy food and supplies from that store.

Bulk products were bought by weight, and the weight was measured in kilograms—Cuba utilized the metric system. For example, families were allowed monthly allotments of 240 grams (about half a pound) of meat (any available meat) per person, two ounces of coffee per person, and one box of matches. Cooking oil was sold in special containers and measured in pounds; the monthly allotment was one pound per person, and each person was allowed two or three eggs for the month. Sometimes, items listed were not available; something seemed to be missing at any given month.

The Castro government was sometimes very cynical. For example, in a speech, Castro indicated the health properties of chocolate and said that chocolate was being made available for the people. A Cuban worker's average monthly income was about US$10 to $13 a month (about 330 Cuban pesos). A non-sugared chocolate bar of about eight ounces cost around 8 Cuban pesos. A police officer's salary was set at twice the average salary of a doctor or engineer. In Cuba, a police officer's salary was more than that of a cabinet minister or a teacher.

One last observation, or perhaps a warning, for those that may not understand what Socialism/Communism does to you, and to individuals, or should I really call it "the collective"? Let's start with a simple example; you buy toothpaste, once you try it you do not like the taste of it, it does not make enough foam, etc., well, in a capitalistic society, you have the choice of not buying it anymore, and if you want to be bullheaded about it, you write a complaint letter to the CEO of the manufacturer. Here is another one; a deodorant, you say that it does work on you, so what to do when there is only one brand, and you know who the manufacturer is, you got it! The government.

In a Socialist environment, the government owns the toothpaste, the deodorant company, etc.; it belongs to "the people," try to complaint about it to the government, is the ONLY toothpaste company in the country! Good luck! You don't like the TV programs, the coffee taste like crap; you can't find a good toilet paper! Everyone gets the same pay, whether the guy next to you works as hard as you do or not, etc., complaint to the government, get it?

Another concept implemented by the new order—Christmas celebrations were no longer allowed. "Religion is the opium of the people" (Karl Marx). There were no presents to buy. My younger sister Zonia remembers a very dismal and discouraging holiday season for the first time in her life. Inez, who had been preparing her trousseau for her upcoming wedding, broke off her engagement.

All private schools were abolished by the time the school year was over. My mother kept Zonia at home the following September at the start of the 1962 school year to prevent her indoctrination by the revolution and also while making preparations to leave the country.

Once a departing family or individual had received exit visas, a government employee went to the person or family's home and took a detailed inventory of all the items inside the home. Items were tagged and entered into an inventory record for that home. My mother had sold the furniture and everything of value and replaced it all with cheap furniture. This included my valuable stamp collection, which she'd sold for fifty dollars. She had no idea of the value of my collection. She did this stealthily at night, always aware of the CDR's vigilance. Once the inventory was completed and recorded, you could not touch anything.

About mid-March 1962, the day for my mother and sisters to leave Cuba arrived. On one's departure date a government employee—not necessarily the same person who took the initial inventory—would bring records of the inventory previously taken and check to make sure that nothing was missing; only what you were wearing could go with you. The penalty, should the government find anything missing from the inventory, including the nails on the walls, was enough to keep you in the country and void your exit visa.[1]

One last farewell and insult came from our revolutionary, indoctrinated family members. My mother and sisters were "honored" by the presence of Caridad, my mother's younger sister, and one of her younger brother Juan's son. Their good-bye and well wishes consisted of wishing that an atomic bomb would fall on the United States, specifically in Connecticut—Zonia was very afraid, believing this might actually happen—for being traitors to the revolution. My mother threw them out of the apartment.

Finally, my family made it out of the hellhole that Cuba had become and arrived in Miami. There were no direct flights to Connecticut, so they stayed with my uncle Enrique for a few days. This really helped because I had to find a bigger apartment for us. My friend Emilio came to my rescue. Once more, he alerted me to an apartment that had become vacant in the same Victorian building he lived in. The apartment was on the third floor. Of course, George was not too happy about me moving out of Wall Street; we'd had many wild parties in that apartment. But hey, life must go on.

I had another testimony of American generosity. The people who worked with me in my department at K of C were all aware of my background and my efforts to get my mother and sisters out of Cuba. By the time my family arrived from Miami, I had bags of clothing for them, many of them brand-new; food supplies; and even money to help my family and me get ourselves established. That these people had offered help, even though my mother and sisters were total strangers was overwhelming to my family and me; it demonstrated a lot about the American character.

Around the end of July 1962, I received a letter from my Saint Augustine schoolmate and friend Julio Gonzalez. His letter was sent via Mr. George Hyatt Sr. The letter gave me a little insight into the struggles of some of my friends in Cuba during the days of the invasion in April 1961; it went like this:

Denver, July 1962
Dear friend Desi:
I pray to God that, at the receipt of this letter, you are well and in the company of your mother and sisters.
Let me tell you that I arrived in the US on May 9, and I stayed in Miami until my wife gave birth to my son. Can you imagine? I am a father already of a beautiful boy. (He looks just like me, so you know he is absolutely

beautiful.) Today, he turns a month old. On June 28, I was relocated through the Methodist Church to the city of Denver, where I have resided ever since. Everybody has been great to us.

I am now working in a mortgage and loan company as an assistant accountant. I made friends with the boss, and he drives me home every day.

While in Cuba, I received, a returned letter that I had sent you marked on front "Unknown Person at this Address." I did not know why, since I had no news that you had moved. I honestly thought that you were again getting involved in another invasion attempt.

Let me tell you that of the people with whom I was doing counterrevolutionary work, two have been put through the firing squad. The other one was given thirty years. I and another companion were able to escape with our skin on, and we made it here. During the invasion, the authorities searched my house from one end to the other, but they were not able to find anything that would compromise me, so they let me go. Unfortunately for the others, they were able to find evidence, so we could not do anything for them.

Through Mr. Hyatt and my brother Calixto (who, by the way, is here with me and my mother in Denver; thank God that my family is all together), we have learned that you are working like a horse, but that is good. The important thing is to be able to eat.

Well, Desi, I hope you can send me a postcard. My best regards to your mom and sisters. I leave you with a strong embrace from your bother in Christ,

Julio.

The remainder of 1962 and 1963 went by very quickly; we were just being acclimated to the new temperatures and culture. I was doing very well at work. I was being promoted, and earning more money; I worked overtime at K of C whenever offered.

I bought my first car, a 1956 Isetta (manufactured by BMW). It looked like an egg. The door opened up front, and the steering went with the door when it opened. It only seated two passengers and got about 75 miles to the gallon. It was always breaking. My second car was a 1959 Taunus station wagon (manufacture by Ford-Germany), a much better car.

I was even recommended as a very good and accurate IBM machine operator to Applied Data Processing, a computer service company not too far from the K of C headquarters. I worked part-time for the computer service for many years. Also on weekends, Fred and I alternated cleaning and maintaining a bowling alley located in a nearby town, Hamden.

Then, one day, out of the clear blue sky, during my lunchtime, sometime in August 1963, I was holding my tray looking at my lunch choices at the K of C cafeteria and picking as much as food as I could eat—I was still trying to gain some weight. I heard a voice behind my back.

"Hi, how are you?"

I turned around to see who it was. A beautiful, blonde, blue-eyed girl with a big, beautiful smile was looking at me.

"Good. How are you?" I responded.

"You are new here, aren't you?" I added after taking a good look at her.

"Yeah, I just graduated from high school; I hope I can start college next semester." She gave me all this information while we were moving along the line.

"My, you got a big tray there," she said smilingly and pointing to my tray.

"Yeah, I'm trying to gain some weight," I said while paying for my lunch.

"Do you mind if I sit with you?" she said.

My first wife Ronaele, sister Zonia, and my mother. Taken in front of the Church where we were married in 1967, West Haven, Conn., circa 1966.

At first, I did not know what to say. My friends from my department were looking at us. I chose a table a little distance from my friends; I did not want them to start fooling around with me.

"So ... what is your name?" she asked, starting the conversation with a smile on her face.

"Desi Sanchez," I replied. "And yours?"

"You mean like Desi Arnaz?" she asked. This type of introduction had been following me all the days of my life.

"Yeah, something like that," I responded.

"Ronaele Coe—that's my name—but my friends call me Ronnie," she responded.

"Coe, what kind of last name is that," I asked.

"My dad is Swedish, and my mother is English. My mother's name is Eleanor, so she named me with her name spelled backward. Where do you live?" She responded and asked the question in the same breath.

"That is really cool. I live here in New Haven on Whaley Avenue, not too far from work, and you?" I replied.

"I live on Second Avenue in West Haven," she answered.

"Oh wow, are you anywhere near Jimmy's at the Rock?"

"Yeah, about ten minutes away," Ronnie answered, still smiling.

We talked through our whole lunch hour about people, school, work, and her future school plans. We were interrupted by a bell indicating that lunchtime was over.

"Do you want to get together tomorrow for lunch, Ronnie?"

"You betcha!" she responded with a wide smile.

A song from the Temptations, "My Girl," summarized my feelings about meeting Ronnie at that time:

I've got sunshine on a cloudy day
When it's cold outside ...

Ronnie and I were married on August 18, 1967; I became the father of three absolutely beautiful girls.

What else could I possibly ask for?

Epilogue

I still remembered the conversation that I'd had with Robert years ago on board DDE *Eaton* about his plans after leaving the navy. In essence, he was referring to what is known as the American dream. Well, I believe that I achieved that dream, my way. The dream is not necessarily about becoming wealthy or something like that. I also think that the American dream is about achieving personal success at whatever you are good at. I did get good jobs; I did get married, had children, and had a house, although I did not have the white picket fence. Not too bad.

After settling in Connecticut, I worked very hard for the next eighteen years. I strived to excel in my profession and to get as a far as I could. I became an experienced programmer. Then I moved up to senior programmer analyst, and eventually I became an IT manager and ran my own department.

My children were all grown up. Tara, my oldest was attending Brigham Young University. Ilana and Danielle had graduated from high school and were in the process of finding their own way in life.

My daughters, left to right; Ilana, Danielle and Tara.

By 1985, Ronnie and I were divorced, a very traumatic

experience, not just for my children but for me as well. Everything happens for a reason, I guess. I started my personal life again. I tried to be as busy as much as I could. I spent as much time with my children as possible, and I kept myself accessible to them at all times. One morning, a radio announcement called my attention, and I joined an organization that catered to divorced parents (Parents Without Partners).

My mother was getting older; for many years, I had spent very little time with my family in Florida. I thought change would do me good; eventually I moved to Miami, and I kept an active membership in the PWP.

One evening in 1991, at PWP, and while enjoying my favorite pastime, dancing, I met my beautiful wife to be; Marty. I asked her to dance, and we seemed to click. Over time, we realized our compatibility, and we were married in July 1992.

Not that I was thinking about this every day, but from 1961 to 1994, I often wondered what had become of my neighborhood friends and schoolmates. How were they doing under Castro's Communism? Were they still alive?

Why 1994? I cannot remember exactly what month or day it happened, but out of nowhere, I met, while

My wife Martha, taken in Connecticut, 2003.

shopping in a food market, of all people; Eduardo Castellon. Yes sir, Gudelia's driver. Together, we were able to gather closed to two hundred Saint Augustine graduates. We formed an incorporated association, and I became its second president. I also found my best friend, Evelio; he had become a mechanical engineer and was running his own business. His own struggle in Cuba could actually become a book.

My mother lived by herself in a separate apartment behind my sister Zonia's house. My father had passed away in Cuba back in the late 1980s from emphysema. I and my two sisters were working. My mother had already fallen several times inside her apartment. We were all very worried. Concerned that her condition would only get worse, we agreed that she needed to be under twenty-four-hour care. We researched and found a very reputable nursing home for her, near Zonia's house.

My father visiting from Cuba to meet his grandchildren for the first time. Photo taken in 1985.

My mother was very independent, and she always loved her privacy. Every time I visited her at the nursing home, she would ask me to take her back to her apartment. Of course she could not return to the apartment; she was already in a wheelchair, but just to make her feel better, I would tell her that as soon as she got better, I would take her home.

Her birthday came up, and I did not realize it. No one in my family called me to remind me either, so I did not make it to her birthday party. I felt real bad and guilty at the same time. I was told that she had a great time with everybody around her and that she really enjoyed the cake brought to her. The following morning, I received a call from the nursing home telling me that my mother had passed away at 5:00 a.m. on the morning of January 31, 2001.

My mother receiving her American citizenship, 1998.

My mother had written a poem early in December 1999, and she wanted me to type it and give it to her. I translated the poem to English; allow me to share it with you:

Between Young and Old
Between young and old
We have know the cause
In regard to each of us
Women, that, we end up alone.
Between young and old
We all had a life,
Beautiful and filled with laughter and dreams
And all the beautiful things that God gave us
To adore and take care of.
Between young and old
Let's remember then, since we were children
We grew like a flower,
First the bud, then the petals,
Perfumed like a colorful rose.
Today we are aged,
For I do not like to say old,
Like broken pieces of old furniture we are set aside,
We think and accept.
Being old, let's give thanks to God
With a smile as to when we were young,
Let's give thanks.

I experienced what I and some of my friends thought was a funny episode, but first I must layout the circumstances that led to the "funny" incident.

I was employed at APPI, a manufacturing company, and my two-year project was coming to an end; it was time to start looking for a new job. Miami was not like Connecticut, where my expertise was in great demand. In Miami, the field of expertise in demand, as far as the computer field in general, was quite different.

Okay, this is the setup. My employment agent procured me an interview with the IT department director of a company called Windmere's (which is no longer in existence). Prior to my interview, I had spoken to the human resources director. I'd informed him that, since my interview was during my lunch hour and my current company's dress code was casual, I would be dressed casually. He told me that wouldn't be an issue.

My interview started the usual way; the IT director questioned me about my current employer, what applications systems I had worked with, which computer languages I was proficient in, what my goals were, and so on. Of course, I answered all of his questions. Then it was his turn to tell me a little about the company, the system, his expectations, and the like. Now, this was where it got a little weird. He paused and looked at me, and then he said, "You know, you look very relaxed, laid back, like you are on vacation. This job is not an eight-to-five job. You may have to work overtime, and somehow, I get the impression that you are not the type to work very hard." Blah, Blah, Blah. He ranted for a while.

My response was this; first, I looked at him in silence with an incredulous look on my face. By the expression on my face, I clearly showed him that I could not believe what I was hearing, and then I turned my head around toward the human resources director, who was sitting next to me, and I directed my response to him. "You led me to believe that wearing a Hawaiian shirt to this interview was not going to be an issue," I told him. "I clearly mentioned that to you. Furthermore, I also said that I was going to come during my lunch break and that my attire conformed to my company's dress code. It appears to me that your IT director is categorizing me according to my shirt and not according to my experience or the expertise that I could bring to the IT department of this company."

That was not all; I continued without being interrupted. "I have worked in this field for over thirty-five years, and I have also worked countless overtime hours. I have worked for companies that are just as good as this one. It seems to me that this interview is about over. I am not sure that I want to work for this director," I concluded, pointing at the IT director.

I got up, and the human resources director and I walked out of his office together.

Wait! Don't close the book yet! I am getting to it, just be a little patient.

I was really lucky; I found a very good job shortly after my project was completed at APPI as a senior programmer analyst at an aircraft service company, dedicated to fueling and airport ground services. I worked for ASIG for five years, until it was sold out two times. The second time, the purchaser moved the company out of Miami, and it merged it with its parent company.

During the second purchase of ASIG, I contacted my faithful employment agent; of course he was always ready to help me out. I think he was working on his second BMW, due to the commissions he'd earned via my job changes.

So what do you think that happened to me? Do you believe that, at this point, I was caught off guard and left out in the cold? No way, Jose, not me!

Anyway, my agent called me back much sooner than I'd thought. "Hey, Desi! I got a great interview for you. This company, Applica, is looking for a senior programmer analyst, and I believe it is a perfect match for your experience." He then gave me the day and time of my interview.

I went to the interview at the appointed time and hour. When I arrived, the building looked very familiar to me. *Why do I think that have I been here before?* I asked myself. The company name wasn't familiar. Well, probably a different company has moved to this building, I concluded.

Surprise! The human resources director was the same man who had interviewed me five years ago. For some reason, he did not remember me at all. Windmere was now Applica! I went through the usual interview steps. Then the HR director said that the IT department director was going to interview me next. *Oh God,* I said to myself, *not the same guy who didn't hire me because I was wearing a Hawaiian shirt.*

Good Lord, almighty! Could someone shout me an Alleluia?

The IT director was not the same man who I had encountered five years ago. Whew, that was close!

The interview with the new IT director went very well. He asked me the appropriate questions, and I answered to his satisfaction. I was hired. Then he said that I would normally meet his boss, the COO, but unfortunately, he was out on vacation. He told me the COO's name. He was the same guy who had interviewed me five years earlier—yes, sir, the one who'd had an issue with my Hawaiian shirt. *Gulp!*

So … what happened when the COO came back from his vacation, and he was introduced to all the new employees, including me? *Nothing.* He just did not remember me at all; the gods were with me!

About a year later, there was a reorganization at Applica, and my nemesis, the COO, was let go. Karma is going to get you! A few months later, the COO was just a memory, I related that story to a couple of my coworkers at Applica. Of course, they could not believe it.

In 2004, I retired from Applica, after forty-three years in the computer field. I wrote close to nine hundred programs, held the position of IT director for two companies, learned and programmed in nine different languages, supported and maintained six proprietary systems packages, operated ten different brands of computer equipment, and changed companies twelve times. I guess I was not too faithful to any of these companies. From that point of view, I was looking out for myself.

Marty and I have been married for twenty years, and we are still dancing. Her daughter, Ana, had a daughter named Amanda, and Amanda has just turned twenty-one. My daughter Ilana was blessed with a very handsome son, finally a boy in my family! My grandson, Devin, was born in August 2000. My daughter Danielle had a beautiful girl name Rayna; my granddaughter was born in May 2011. Tara is still single and living and working in Salt Lake City. Marty Jr. is also single, and she is pursuing a successful singing career. My sister Inez had a daughter and, following with tradition, her little girl was named after our grandmother, Inez. My sister Zonia has two boys, Daniel and Michael. Daniel is an artist, and he is married. Michael was a musician but eventually became a computer expert. He is also married.

So what else is coming our way? Who knows? Is this the end, or is it just the beginning?

Notes

PROLOGUE

[1] Saint Augustine College, established in 1903, was a school for boys administered by the American Augustinian Order. Its commerce curriculum prepared the students to either continue to seek higher education at the University of Havana or at the prestigious Augustinian Villanova University, which also functioned in Cuba, or to seek employment at the many corporate offices established in Havana. The Saint Augustine College building and grounds are situated in the old section of Havana and have the distinction of having one of the oldest churches built (circa 1500s) by the Spaniards in the Americas. Before moving out to the suburbs, my family and I lived about two and half blocks away from the school.

CHAPTER 1: CRUSHES AND CRASHES

[1] The church was built in a plaza named after the church, Cristo del Buen Viaje (Christ of the Good Voyage). Plaza del Cristo and its existence are entered in the Cabildo Act of March 13, 1640. The church was the second built during Colonial times. After the Spanish American War in 1900, Spain lost its colony to the Americans. Cuba became a Republic in 1902. In the following year, the American Augustinians from the Philadelphia Province took charge of the church, to provide services to a growing American colony in Cuba. In 1903, the Santo Cristo Parish started and eventually founded Saint Augustine College

[2] OSA is the *Ordo Sancti Augustini* (Order of Saint Augustine). In 1999, a movement started to submit to the Vatican the name of Father John McKniff, OSA, for beatification. If canonized, Father Mckniff would be one of the few American Saints. During the early days of the revolution, the government closed the school and all of the Augustinian fathers (with the exception of Father John McKniff, OSA) were expelled from Cuba. Today, the park across

191

from the school and the church buildings has been integrated. Buses or cars can no longer travel in front of the buildings.

[3] The Augustinian Order had been connected with Cuba since 1608, when the order established the first convent in the Caribbean. The order arrived in Havana with the intention of also creating an Augustinian community to house other transient Augustinians commuting from Spain and the West Indies. The Augustinian Order consists of primarily teachers. There are no longer any Augustinians (Spanish or American) in Cuba today.

[4] Saint Augustine's curriculum consisted of religion, accounting and bookkeeping, business arithmetic, business calculus, shorthand (English and Spanish,) typing (English and Spanish), algebra, businesses calligraphy, English (advanced and business), commerce geography, and history of commerce.

[5] During the Batista government, from 1952–1959, "Fidelistas," terrorist and rebel groups, were increasing their indiscriminate bombings and violence around Havana and its suburbs. The bombings were terrorist tactics designed to disrupt our daily lives and hurt normal business activity, thus creating a feeling of insecurity. By around 1957, due to these increased bombings and rebel activity, the Batista government suspended constitutional guarantees. My school friends and I were members of the Felix Varela Columbian Squires, Circle #612, and we were located in Santos Suarez and La Vibora suburbs of Havana. Because of the suspended constitutional guaranties, we could not get a permit from the local authorities to conduct our meetings. It became more difficult for us to seek new members, participate in social affairs, and perform the typical duties of an organization. We had to conduct our meetings without official permits, running the risk of being caught by the police and being carted off to jail or worse—like falling into the hands of the secret police or the military intelligence service. We believed that the previously described authorities had been pressured to show progress against terrorist and pro-Castro activist and sympathizers. One of the ways to show progress was to have a body count of a prescribed, implied, or imaginary quota of killed or captured revolutionaries or even suspected revolutionaries. Due to these challenges, our group was reduced to about eight members.

CHAPTER TWO: ROCK 'N ROLL, GRADUATION, AND GIRLS

[1] Years later, sometime in 1964, when I was living in New Haven, Connecticut, I bought a 1956 Buick Roadmaster from one of my coworkers' mother's. It was in great shape, baby blue and white inside and outside; it was too big for me! One evening, I went out to buy pizza. On the way back, I was stopped by a police officer. "What did I do?" I asked. "Let me see your license, please." The officer checked my license, smiled, and told me, "Okay, I stopped you because I thought you were a teenager out for a joyride. This car is too big for you." I never really looked my age. I think owning a 1956 Buick was a special thing for me, even if it was too big!

[2] Before automation, conductors had the job of collecting the bus fare, providing transfers, and advising the driver when a passenger had reached his destination and needed to make a stop at the designated stop. (Today, bus drivers do all that.) Many times, the driver would slow down just enough for you to jump off the bus, recommended for young people only.

[3] Gudelia was a 1955 Renault 4CV, named so after Eduardo's grandmother.

[4] Nat King Cole, inspired by a trip to Havana, Cuba, in 1958, returned that same year and recorded *Cole Español*, an album sung entirely in Spanish and Portuguese. The album was a hit not only in the United States but in Latin America as well.

Chapter 3: Who Took My Prostitutes Away?

[1] General Antonio Maceo Grajales was second in command of the Cuban Army of Independence. Commonly known as "the Titan of Bronze," Maceo was one of the outstanding guerrilla leaders in nineteenth century Latin America, easily comparable to José Antonio Páez of Venezuela. The son of a Venezuelan mulatto and an Afro-Cuban woman, Maceo began his fight for Cuban liberation by enlisting as a private in the army in 1868 when the Ten Years War began. Five years later, he was promoted to the rank of general because of his bravery and his demonstrated ability to outmaneuver the Spanish Army. In 1878, when most of the Cubans generals believed that their armies could not defeat the Spaniards, Maceo refused to surrender without winning Cuban independence and the abolition of slavery. Ultimately, he was forced to leave Cuba. He returned to Cuba when war with Spain began again. His most famous campaign in the War of Cuban Liberation was his invasion of western Cuba, when his troops, mostly Afro-Cubans on horseback, covered more than a thousand miles in ninety-two days and fought the enemy in twenty-seven separate encounters. Spanish General Valeriano Weyer pursued him vigorously, if only to curtail Maceo's destruction of the Cuban sugar industry. On December 7, 1896, Maceo was captured and killed as he attempted to rejoin Maximo Gomez's forces. His death prompted yet another congressional resolution for belligerent rights for Cuba.

[2] *Jineteras*—In Spanish a *jinete* is an equestrian, horseman, or jockey. *Jinetera* is female for the given definition. It obviously means that she will mount "you" for a price.

[3] In *The New Class*, circa 1956, Czech author Milovan Djilas expounds on the "new class" created by the Communist elite, who do not, among other things, lack power or any of life's "little" pleasures.

Chapter 4: Deceit, Breakup, and a New Year's Nightmare

[1] Faure Chomon was one of the young men who were in the group that participated in the Presidential Palace attack. I believe that he was also sent to Moscow in the capacity of the Cuban ambassador to the Soviet Union in the early sixties.

Chapter 6: A New Sheriff in Town

[1] This explanation went out the window when Fidel declared, in 1962, that he was a follower of Lenin's and Marx's doctrine and that he was going to establish a "socialist" state based on his "Revolution," thus creating a single political party.

[2] When this process was completed, Castro had nationalized billions of dollars (in today's dollars) worth of American-owned businesses. At that time, this made the Eisenhower government in Washington very mad.

[3] Born in Montenegro, Milovan joined the Communist party of Yugoslavia in 1932 and fought along Tito's side as a partisan against German occupation. After World War II, he became a vice president in Tito's government and established the Socialist Federal Republic of Yugoslavia. He came into disgrace when he wrote several articles demanding more democracy in the party and in the country. In 1955, he published *The New Class: An Analysis of the Communist System*, in which he argued that Communists in Eastern Europe were not promoting equality in political, social, and civil rights as promoted by their beliefs. He spent nine years in prison and then went to prison again in 1962. Despite his dissident views, he still thought of himself as a Communist. He was also opposed to the breakup of Yugoslavia.

[4] By early 1960, what was thought to be the promise of the revolution started to become undone for many of us. Several groups took for the mountains of Escambray, the same spot where my uncle Francisco had fought as a rebel against Batista just a couple of years earlier. Francisco told me that there were also other groups in the west, Pinar del Rio Province, and in the east, Oriente Province. According to 1997 documents released by CIA under the FOIA, there were drops of weapons, propaganda, food, and supplies run by the CIA in these provinces and locations during the last few months of 1960. Eventually, Castro extinguished these groups.

Chapter 7: Looking for a Way Out

[1] It did not take long for the people to realize that it was a bad deal; you could not sell or trade the property given to you because the "government was the real owner."

[2] The CIA was already conducting clandestine operations in Cuba. On September 28, an airdrop of a one hundred-man arms pack was dropped for an agent rated as having potential as a resistance leader. The crew missed the drop zone by several miles; the package was dropped on a dam. Castro forces scooped up the package and immediately surrounded the area, captured the agent, and shot him.

[3] Agents of the CDR (Committee for the Defense of the Revolution) were set up in every neighborhood and apartment building—anywhere people lived. The purpose of the CDR was not the same as the US's Neighborhood Crime Watch. CDR members were to spy on their neighbors and report anything they thought unusual or suspicious. The committee idea was modeled after the East Germany committees ran by the East German Secret Police during the Soviet occupation. The committees opened the door, I am sure, for some people to settle personal issues as well.

[4] The name of the ship was the SS *Houston*, an old World War II Liberty type merchant ship owned by the Garcia Line. Besides an office in Havana, the Garcia Line had its main office in New York.

CHAPTER 8: MY MERCHANT MARINE CARD AND SOMETHING EXTRA

[1] I later found out from my uncle that the Garcia Line was extracting people from Cuba who were involved in the counterrevolution. Maybe that is how I was able to get a job there. I never found out for sure.

[2] When my mother and sisters finally made it to the United States in 1962, she told me that the last time she went to pick up the money, a few weeks after the invasion, the militia men had intervened in the lumber company and taken it away from the owners. Matias kept his word and gave my mother my earnings every week. I thought that was fantastic. I never saw him again. I would have like to thank him one more time.

CHAPTER 9: BYE-BYE, HAVANA

[1] El Paseo del Prado was a two-way boulevard, in the center of which was a wide walkway adorned with wavy tiles and rows of huge, beautiful laurel trees on both sides of the walkway, along with many sidewalks cafés. Every year, the famous Havana Carnivals were held along this boulevard. High school bands from Miami came to march and play here during the carnival time in March.

[2] La Rampa was located in El Vedado, a kind of entertainment complex. It hosted a movie theater, radio and TV stations, restaurants, nightclubs, and related small offices and services. The Havana Hilton was less than a block away, as well as the Havana University; this area was very busy traffic wise.

[3] The FOCSA (Fomentos de Obras y Construcciones SA) is considered one of the marvels of Cuban engineering. Built in record time, just twenty-eight months, the FOCSA is located on a square block between 17, 19, M, and N streets in El Vedado. Construction began on February 1954, and the building was completed in June 1956. The building has thirty-nine floors, thirty floors for apartments and nine floors for multiple uses, including a movie theater, stores, supermarket, and even a TV studio. The building, 397 feet high, was made of concrete and, at the time, was the second tallest concrete building in the world. The typical floor has thirteen apartments, five apartments with thirteen bedrooms and maid's quarters and eight with bedrooms and maid's quarters. The three-bedroom corner apartments had a price of 21,500 pesos, and the other ones were 17,500 pesos each. The price would go up 30 pesos for each higher floor.

CHAPTER 10: A GREAT TIME IN NEW ORLEANS?

[1] *Sobrino* is Spanish for nephew.

[2] *Tío* is Spanish for uncle.

[3] Every year, during early March, the famous Havana Carnivals were held along El

Paseo del Prado boulevard. On Fridays neighborhood conga bands competed with their costumes, and their music. On Saturdays, High school bands from Miami came to march and play. Floats representing different themes rode along the boulevard, and of course the presentation of the Carnival Queen.

Chapter 11: Choosing between Life and Death

[1] The Houston was a Liberty type vessel. The original WWII Liberty ships had several machines guns installed at strategic places throughout the ship.

[2] The crew members of the SS *Houston* were still employees of Garcia Lines. Puerto Cabezas was the destination, the end of the line, to make the final decision of joining the fight or remaining in Nicaragua until it was over. A very small group of the *Houston* crew decided to remain in Nicaragua, some of them because of the fear of the danger that was to face them, others because of sympathy with the Castro regime. The great majority decided to take the same risk as the brigadiers and contributed to what we believed was to be the beginning of the Cuban liberation from a Communist System.

[3] I understood how very absent a plan B was when I read a memorandum dated December 1, 1961, from Inspector General Lyman B. Kirkpatrick to the director of the CIA. ("Report of the Cuban Operation," FOIA, paragraphs a., b., and c.) a. An overall lack of recognition on the part of the US Government as to the magnitude of the operation required to overthrow the Fidel Castro regime. b. The failure on the part of the US Government to plan for all contingencies at the time of the Cuban operation including the necessity for using regular US military forces in the event that exiled Cubans could not do the job themselves. c. The failure on part of the US Government to be willing to commit to the Cuban operation, as planned and executed, those necessary resources required for its success.

[4] In my own opinion, today there is a danger that nonaligned countries not friendly to the United States will attempt to establish, in the near future, weapons of mass destruction on Cuban soil as a direct threat to America, pretty much like the October 1962 Cuban Missile Crisis. On September 14–16, 2006, there was a meeting in Havana with Iran, Syria, North Korea, Venezuela and thirty-six other countries to form alliances against the United States. History has a way of repeating itself when inappropriate actions were taken.

Chapter 12: Right behind My Back

[1] LCIs (Landing Craft, Infantry) were assault ships used during World War II. LCUs (Landing Craft, Utility) were used to transport troops and equipment to shore. LCVPs (Landing Craft, Vehicle, Personal) were used for amphibious landings.

[2] I did not know this at the time, but many of my friends from Saint Augustine College were in training at the Guatemalan camps, including my good friend German Koch, who was a paratrooper and was killed during the invasion by the Cubans before he even hit the ground.

Chapter 13: Sailing for Nicaragua

[1] I really sweated out this five-dollar bill. I had decided about six months before this *Houston* business to study architectural design at a very well-known private school in Havana, Instituto Garces; private schools would soon disappear. While I was going to work at the port where the *Houston* was anchored and being repaired, I placed the five-dollar bill somewhere toward the end of my architectural math book, and I took it to the ship with me every day. The revolutionary guard (militiaman) at the port never looked in my book. The penalty for being in possession of American dollars at that time was heavy.

[2] I believe that Doctor Rene Lamar took care of Osvaldo. The doctor was later seriously wounded on the *Houston* while we were under attack by Castro's air force.

Chapter 14: Midnight Fireworks, No Fiesta

[1] Cuban Brigade 2506—The CIA Cuban assault force was composed entirely of Cuban volunteers. They trained for action in a Guatemalan camp as a heavily armed, hard-hitting military unit. One of the early brigadiers, Carlos R. Santana, died during training exercises. His serial number was 2506, and the brigade took his serial number, thus becoming Assault Brigade 2506. By the time the invasion commenced there were about 1,500 combatants.

[2] In late 1960, the project leaders were becoming doubtful of the motivation of the Cuban pilots they were training and of their ability to perform tactical missions successfully. In January 1961, the CIA requested the special group to authorize the use of American contract pilots. The special group also granted authority to recruit and hire American seamen to serve in the invasion fleet. Three American contract pilots with long agency experience were made available. A number of other pilots and aircrew technicians, members or ex-members of several Air National Guard units, were recruited especially for the project in early 1961 under cover of a national commercial company. (Source FOIA—Inspector General's Survey of the Cuban Operation, "Americans in Combat.")

[3] The CIA had bought the *Barbara J*, an LCI, in October 1960. It was originally intended as a mother ship for small boats operations and long-range lift capabilities. The *Barbara J* and the *Blagar* (another LCI) were purchased in Miami for $70,000 but after repairs and modifications, the cost was $253,000. The *Barbara J* was to land troops on Red Beach, as well as carry the Cuban elite frogmen or UDTs (Underwater Demolition Team).

[4] Anastacio Somoza was the president of Nicaragua and general of the Nicaraguan Army at that time. He was eventually deposed by the Castro-inspired Nicaraguan Revolution of Daniel Ortega.

[5] Radio Swan (source, FOIA ANNEX A March 16, 1961)—Transmission of opposition views had already begun. Private individuals had purchased commercial

time to broadcast oppositions views from Miami, arrangements had been made with station WRUL for additional broadcast from Massachusetts (short wave) and from Florida (broadcast band)) [Censured] and [censured] have also agreed to the use of commercial stations for short wave broadcast from [censured] and [censured]. CIA has furnished support to these efforts through encouragement, negotiating help and providing some broadcast material. As the major voice of opposition, it is proposed to establish at least one "gray" US-controlled station. This will probably be on Swan Island and will employ both high frequency and broadcast band equipment of substantial power. The preparation of scripts will be done in the US, and these will be transmitted electronically to the site for broadcasting.

[6] Preinvasion bombing of Castro's air force—Several B-26s piloted by Cuban pilots, the planes wearing FAR insignias (Revolutionary Air Force), were supposed to decimate, if not destroy, Castro's air force capability. Radio Swan was reporting that the "Cuban Air Force" had rebelled against the Castro government and was carrying an attack against military installation, reporting many deaths and wounded. Of course, the objective of broadcasting misinformation was to confound and confuse the enemy and to help infiltrators already inside Havana and other parts of the island to do their job more effectively. Unfortunately, there were other airplanes in their hangars that were actually in good working condition and ready to fly; two B-26 bombers, two Sea Furys and two T-33 training jets, fully armed. Later, U-2 photographs verified this fact. This "little detail" would spell the end of the invasion plans and assure our defeat. Radio Swan was used during the days on the Bay of Pigs Invasion to send coded messages to insiders and to misinform the Castro military. The Cuban government did not have the sophisticated equipment need it to jam Radio Swan.

CHAPTER 15: SITTING DUCKS

[1] The closest thing I've ever heard to the noise the airplane's bullets made when they hit the *Houston* iron sides was during the first twenty-minute scene of *Saving Private Ryan*. The scene shows the American forces disembarking at Omaha Beach, and the German bullets are hitting the iron defensive and obstacle posts planted by the shore.

[2] (Source, CIA FOIA—Inspector General Survey of the Cuban Operation N "Americans in Combat," pgs. 140–142)—Two American fliers volunteered to go, and several Cuban crews followed their example. The result was a highly successful attack against a column of Castro's forces moving on Blue Beach. Four American-manned aircraft were in combat over the beachhead the following day, and Castro's T33s shot two of them down. Four American fliers were either killed in combat or executed by Castro forces after being shot down. The American pilots lost in combat were aware of the US Government sponsorship and probably also of agency interest, but had been instructed not to inform their families of this. The resolution in a secure manner of the legal and moral claims arising from these four deaths has been costly, complicated, and fraught with risk of disclosure of the government's role.

[3] Phases of the Operation (source, FOIA ANNEX D—Revised Cuban Operation,

March 15, 1961, TS#176622.)—The operation will begin with a night landing. There are no known enemy forces (even police) in the objective area, and it is anticipated that the landing can be carried out with few if any casualties and with no serious combat. As many supplies as possible will be unloaded over the beaches, but the ships will be put to sea in time to be well offshore by dawn.

CHAPTER 17: WE HAVE TO GET OUT OF HERE

[1] So far, our tally was not too good. The air attacks from Castro's supposedly decimated air force continued throughout the day. The eleven B-26s of the brigade's air force, which was supposed to be available for close support, were no match for the T-33 jets. At least four of Castro's aircraft were shot down by our ship's machine guns and by friendly air support. The first wave of ground attacks by Castro's militia occurred at Red Beach in the morning, afternoon, and evening of the seventeenth. While the ammunition lasted, these attacks were repealed, with heavy militia casualties; several of Castro's tanks were damaged or destroyed by ground and friendly action. On the morning of the eighteenth, Red Beach brigadiers were out of ammunition. They moved on to Blue Beach without any pressure from the enemy. In addition to supporting ground forces and protecting the ships, friendly B-26s also sank a Castro patrol escort ship and attacked the Cienfuegos Airfield. Four of the friendly B-26s were shot down, while three returned safely to Nicaragua and four landed at other friendly bases. Resupplying the brigadiers by the sea was cancelled due to obvious reasons. On the night of the seventeenth and the eighteenth, one C-54 drop was made at Red Beach and three at Blue Beach. (Source FOIA—Inspector General's Survey of the Cuban Operation.)

[2] At Blue Beach, Castro executed an attack on the brigadiers from three directions supported by their air force. Six friendly B-26s, two of them flown by Americans, inflicted heavy damage on the Castro forces moving to our position from the west; the friendly forces used napalm, bombs, rockets, and machine gun fire to destroy several Soviet Stalin tanks and trucks carrying troops. Castro reported his casualties at about 1,800. The brigade's ability to resist Castro's forces repeated attacks from the west depended on resupplies of ammunitions, which by now had become all but impossible. By the night of April 18, brigadier's commanders refused an offer to evacuate their troops. (Source, CIA FOIA—Inspector General Survey of the Cuban Operation.)

[3] Air support to the Blue Beach troops was continued on the morning of April 19. At that point three friendly B-26s, two of them piloted by Americans, were shot down by Castro's T-33 jets. There was supposed to be jet air cover from the Navy Aircraft Carrier *Essex*; the *Essex* was with their support of about five destroyers and a sub, just outside Cuban waters, and they were expected to support the April 19 sorties against Castro's forces. But a misunderstanding prevented them from executing the support. In the last hours of resistance, the brigade commander sent several terse and desperate messages to the task force command ship pleading for help. "We are out of ammo and fighting on the beach. Please send help. We cannot hold." "In water. Out of ammo. Enemy closing in. Help must arrive in next hour." "When your help will here

and with what?" "Why your help has not come?" The last message was as follows: "Am destroying all equipment and communications. Tanks are in sight. I have nothing to fight with. Am taking to the woods. I cannot repeat cannot wait for you." (Source, CIA FOIA—Inspector General Survey of the Cuban Operation.)

Chapter 18: Getting Weaker

[1] The American Navy and our own Cuban frogmen were already looking for survivors along the coast. Also during this time, Castro's helicopters were looking for survivors. About four of Castro's helicopters were flying along the swamps at low altitude. Two of the helicopters were two-seaters, and the other two were very large Russian helicopters, all painted green, with no markings. Unlike the Americans who were saving survivors, they were hunting survivors. (Source, "After Action Report on Operation Pluto, Doc. 159378," FOIA)

Chapter 19: Among The Dead And The Doomed.

[1] The Ouija—Ouija means "yes, yes"— board was patented in 1891 by a fellow named Elijah J. Bond. The right to the Ouija board was purchased the following year by William Fuld. Until then, there was nothing new about the Ouija board. The board has been around since before Christ's time. It is believe that the board had been around since the time of the Roman Emperor Valens in the fourth century BC, and it was even thought to have been used by the Greeks as well, as a form of divination. A typical Ouija board is a combination of letters of the alphabet arranged in a circle or in the form of a half moon. The numbers, from zero to nine, are arranged opposite of the letters, and the words "yes" and "no" are opposite from one another. The second part of the Ouija is a glass, preferably a wine glass placed inverted on the middle of the board, the board must be slippery so that the glass can slide easily during operation of the board. Ideally, three people should be involved in the usage of the board, two to place their fingertips on the glass. The other person takes notes of the letters, number, and words as the glass glides across the board. The commercial Ouija board provides a plastic "planchette" with a small glass circle and a needle in the middle that points to a letter, number, or word.

Chapter 20: Ours or Theirs?

[1] The destroyer's name was the USS *Conway* DDE-507, (one of the five supporting ships for the aircraft carrier the *Essex*). A few days later, we were transferred somewhere in the Gulf from the *Conway* to the destroyer, USS *Eaton* DDE-510.

[2] When I finally got established in New Haven, Connecticut, I presented myself to the local post office, and I registered with the U S Selective Service. (I kept my SS card as a memento.) I was looking forward to joining the navy. In 1962, a few months shy of the Cuban Missile Crisis, I was able to bring my mother and two sisters from Cuba to the United State. I was recLasified; I was not able to join the navy or any of the armed forces.

[1]What Cubans cannot do—travel out the country; change jobs; change residences without government permission; watch private TV stations (all TV stations are owned and run by the government); read books, newspapers, or magazines, unless approved and published by the government; receive publications from abroad or from visitors (jail terms applied to violators); visit or stay in tourist hotels, restaurants, and resorts (off-limits to Cuban citizens); seek employment with foreign companies on the island, unless approved by the government; run for public office, unless approved by Cuba's Communist party; join an independent labor union (there is only one, government labor union—no strikes, protests, individual or collective bargaining is allowed); retain a lawyer, unless approved by the government; see physicians or go to hospitals not only assigned to you by the government; refuse to participate in mass rallies and demonstration organized by Cuba's Communist party; criticize the Castro government or the Cuban Communist party, the only party allowed. (Source—Cuba Facts.)